DAILY NOTES TO GOD
A DEVOTIONAL EXPERIENCE

BY NOEL PALMER

Cover design by Mark Silverstone.

ISBN: 978-0-9858257-0-6

In loving appreciation,
I dedicate this book to my wife, Daisy,
who is my most discerning critic
and my best friend.

———⬡⬡⬡———

Dear Friends:

Over the years, before I start my day's work,

I often pause and write a note to God.

I now share them with you.

I hope that you will catch a glimpse of the

inspiration I gleaned from the Scriptures and other

devotional writing. I was nurtured by the Spirit

as I reached out each morning.

Noel Palmer

January

JANUARY 1

Dear Heavenly Father:

I thank Thee for a new year with all its promises and hopes. I thank Thee that Thou art in this new year and, indeed, Thou art the Preserver and Sustainer of it. I am confident, O Lord, that with Thee there is all that is good. I ask Thy guidance and care as I once more give myself to Thee. *Amen.*

JANUARY 2

Dear Heavenly Father:

To Thee I give this morning's thanksgiving for all that Thou art to me and to all the world. Thou hast thought of us while we were asleep, and provided for us during our waking moments. Thou art always mindful of us, even more than we could be of ourselves. Help me this day to serve Thee aright. *Amen.*

JANUARY 3

Eternal Father:

Thou hast equipped us with senses to be aware of our environment. Thou hast allowed us to feel the warmth of the sun, the beauty of the sky, the various formations of the clouds. Thou hast allowed us to hear the chirping of the birds and the humming of the bees. Most of all, Thou hast given us the response to Thy love, and so I thank Thee this day. *Amen.*

JANUARY 4

Eternal Father:

It is good to have the assurance of Thy love and guidance, to know that Thou wilt never leave me nor forsake me, and to know that Thou art working Thy purpose out with me in it. Help me, Lord, to be ever mindful of Thy presence and to follow Thy leading. Use me as Thou wilt, I pray. *Amen.*

JANUARY 5

Dear Heavenly Father:
I thank Thee for Thy goodness, Thy love and Thy care. I thank Thee for another opportunity of praising Thy Name. I thank Thee that Thou hast revealed Thyself through Thy Son and my Lord Jesus Christ, and that through Him I have access to Thee. Grant me Thy Holy Spirit who teacheth all truth, and help me to serve Thee aright. *Amen.*

JANUARY 6

Dear Heavenly Lord:
For Thy keeping and Thy care, Thy mercy and Thy goodness, Thy love and Thy grace, I give Thee thanks this day. Bring me into the fullness of Thy plan, and help me to know and do Thy will. Lead me in the path of righteousness and cause me to fulfill Thy purpose. *Amen.*

JANUARY 7

Dear Heavenly Father:
Thou who in Thy wisdom hast given me Thy gifts that Thou knowest I will be in need of, help me to discover the potential of all these blessings so that I can develop them and use them to the honor and glory of Thy Name. Use me this day, I pray. *Amen.*

JANUARY 8

Dear Heavenly Father:
A new day dawns and a fresh supply of Thy blessings is ours. New hope fills our hearts and new joy fills our souls. The knowledge that Thou art our God, and a Preserver and Rewarder of those who come to Thee,

fills us with assurance and praise. Help me this day to show forth Thy love in my life. *Amen.*

JANUARY 9

Eternal Father:

Thou who art strong to save, and to bring the world under Thy charge; Thou who seest the discord and the distrust, the warrings and the wrangling in the world; give us Thy Holy Spirit and lead us into peace. Dear Father, guide me this day and help me to do Thy will, I pray. *Amen.*

JANUARY 10

Father in Heaven:

Thou who art the Giver of peace, the Provider of hope, the Guide of our way, I thank Thee for another day in which I can experience Thy goodness and Thy love. Thou who doest all things well, and who art the Source of all creation, open anew to me this day Thy purpose for my life, and help me to do Thy will. In Thy dear Name, I pray. *Amen.*

JANUARY 11

Eternal Father:

For the consciousness of Thee and the knowledge of Thy marvelous works; for the promises Thou hast given in Thy Word, and in the Word made flesh; dear Father, I thank Thee. Strengthen me in doing that which comes to hand, and bless the effort, that Thy will be done. *Amen.*

JANUARY 12

Eternal Father:

Thou who hast ordained the path through which I lead; Thou who hast been my guide and who hast promised to be with me even unto the end; I thank Thee. Help me to serve Thee aright, and to praise Thy Name in all things. Use me to bring comfort to Thy children and grant us Thy peace. *Amen.*

JANUARY 13

Father in Heaven:
Giver of every good and perfect gift, Thou who hast poured out Thy love toward Thy people, and hast showered us with Thy grace, cause me to rejoice in Thee this day. Help me to really thank Thee for all Thou art, and for all that Thou hast purposed for me. Use me as Thou wilt. *Amen.*

JANUARY 14

Dear Heavenly Father:
Thou who hast led me thus far on my way, and art already beyond the end, I trust Thee for all that Thou hast in store. Make me fit to do that which Thou desirest, and grant me the faith to glorify Thy Name. Help me to abide in Thee as the branch to the vine, and feed me with Thy grace. *Amen.*

JANUARY 15

Eternal Father:
I thank Thee for the meaning of life that Thou givest, for the sense of purpose and the reason for service that Thou allowest. This day that is already fulfilled in Thee, reveal in moments to me, O Lord, so that I may not take one step without Thine aid. Help me in all things to rejoice in Thee. *Amen.*

JANUARY 16

Dear Heavenly Father:

No matter how gloomy the day, I know that it is Thy creation and it comes from the same place and the same hands that fashion the bright and sunny days. Keep my heart centered on Thee today, and help me in all I do to know that I am being led by Thee. Keep me grateful to Thee for all that Thou art to me. *Amen.*

JANUARY 17

Dear Heavenly Father:

Thou who knowest and understandest that which is dearest to us, have Thy way with me this day and let the desires of my heart be acceptable to Thee. Pour out Thy blessings upon me this day and fulfill Thy purpose in me. Dear Lord, let Thy Holy Spirit guide me in the path of truth. *Amen.*

JANUARY 18

Dear Heavenly Father:

As Thy sunlight shines upon me, I am conscious of Thy glorious presence within. I am confident that the illuminating rays of Thy Spirit will guide me throughout this day. Dear Lord, keep me mindful of Thy goodness always, and help me to honor Thee. *Amen.*

JANUARY 19

Dear Heavenly Father:

For a closer walk with Thee, I thank Thee. For the privilege of feeling Thy Spirit within and knowing the joy of Thy comfort, I praise Thee. Help me to grow in Thy grace and to reflect the beauty of Thy peace. Grant me the wisdom to accomplish Thy will in all my doings. Use me, O Lord, I pray. *Amen.*

JANUARY 20

Dear Heavenly Father:
Thou who hast bound us one to another, and hast placed us to benefit from each other; Thou who declarest that it is a good thing for brethren to dwell together in unity; help me to do my part in bringing about peace and good will in this world. Use me in doing Thy will, I pray. *Amen.*

JANUARY 21

Eternal Father:
Thou who art limitless and whose mercy is everlasting, and whose truth endureth to all generations, I thank Thee that Thou art also reliable and that I can trust Thee to work all things out for Thy good. Grant me wisdom this day to honor Thee in my living. In Thy Name I pray. *Amen.*

JANUARY 22

Dear Heavenly Father:
I thank Thee that even when I hit a blank I can still come to Thee. Even when things seem so confusing and I do not even know what to pray for or how to pray, I can come to Thee for comfort, guidance and help. Thou seest the world and knowest our confusion. Help me to love and trust Thee. *Amen.*

JANUARY 23

Eternal Father:
Thou who hast all the possibilities and art ever waiting upon us to come to Thee to receive them; Thou who art ever willing to pour out Thy Spirit upon us; I thank Thee. Help me to abide in Thee and to hold

fast to Thy word, so that I will be guided in the paths of righteousness and peace. *Amen.*

JANUARY 24

Eternal Father:

I thank Thee for the many ways Thou hast given me to praise Thee. I thank Thee that Thou canst satisfy my longing heart with Thy grace. Dear Lord, help me to fully yield to Thy will that Thy purpose will be fulfilled within me. Give me the appropriate words to speak, and the fitting acts to do, that Thy will be done. *Amen.*

JANUARY 25

Dear Heavenly Father:

I thank Thee for all the opportunities that Thou hast given me to make known Thy goodness and Thy love. I thank Thee that Thou hast chosen me to bear witness to Thee. Help me that both my words and my deeds will echo Thy love, and that in all things I will honor Thee. *Amen.*

JANUARY 26

Dear Heavenly Father:

Thou who art the Source of all goodness, and who providest for all our needs; Thou who knowest us within and without, and hast chosen to love us; help me, dear Lord, to respond to Thy love and to yield to Thee my all. Use me as Thou desirest, and cause me in all things to praise Thee. *Amen.*

JANUARY 27

Eternal and Ever-Loving God:

Thou in whose mercies I abide; Thou who constantly pours out Thy love upon me; Thou who art my Keeper and my Guide; I thank Thee,

Lord, for Thy provision and Thy care. I thank Thee that Thou hast chosen me. Use me this day to accomplish Thy will. *Amen.*

JANUARY 28

Dear Heavenly Father:
Giver of life, Preserver of hope, Provider of every good and perfect gift; Thou who hast made a way whereby we can know Thee and give ourselves to Thee; Thou who receivest sinners and art willing to restore us to Thyself; I thank Thee for Thy love. Lead me in the path of righteousness this day, I pray. *Amen.*

JANUARY 29

Dear Heavenly Father:
I thank Thee for all that Thou hast enabled me to do for Thee. I thank Thee that Thou hast shown me more of Thy marvelous creation. I thank Thee for the great possibilities that there are in serving Thee. Grant me the strength, the wisdom, and the will to accomplish that which Thou requirest. *Amen.*

JANUARY 30

Dear Heavenly Father:
Thou who art the Source of our strength, the Anchor of our hope; Thou in whom we confide, for Thou knowest the secrets of our hearts; I thank Thee for always being available and always ready to hear and answer our pleas. Guide me this day, O Lord, and help me in all things to honor Thee. *Amen.*

January 31

Eternal Father:

Thou who givest eternal peace, who settlest every aching heart with Thy Holy Word; Thou who hast said, come unto Me all ye who are heavy laden and I will refresh you; I thank Thee for Thy promise and for the relief I receive when I accept Thy truth. Breathe again Thy Holy Spirit within me this day and help me to live for Thee. *Amen.*

FEBRUARY

FEBRUARY 1

Dear Heavenly Father:
Thou hast opened the door of knowledge and truth to us. Thou who art the Source of all wisdom, help me to know Thee and to do Thy bidding. Grant me that peace which passeth all understanding, and give me courage in doing that which is difficult but right in Thy sight. *Amen.*

FEBRUARY 2

Eternal Father:
For all Thy blessings I give Thee thanks. Thy mercy is everlasting, and Thy truth endures from generation to generation. Thou art always mindful of Thy people, and art always ready to answer our call. Help me this day to walk with Thee and do Thy will. *Amen.*

FEBRUARY 3

Dear Heavenly Father:
Thou who teachest us through all happenings, and hast promised to be with us even unto the end of the world, I thank Thee, Lord, that I can trust Thee. At times I cannot understand what is happening, but, dear Lord, I trust Thee. I am, therefore, comforted to know that all things work together for good with those who trusteth Thee. *Amen.*

FEBRUARY 4

Dear Heavenly Father:
I thank Thee for friends, for people who show forth their love and who help me to know in a tangible way that Thou hast helped me to do what is meaningful and important to them. Continue to use me to spread joy in the lives of Thy children, and grant me wisdom. *Amen.*

FEBRUARY 5

Dear Heavenly Father:
I thank Thee, O Lord, for a new day and for the possibilities that Thou hast packed into this day. I am conscious of Thy Holy Spirit within me to guide me. Use Thy Spirit to gain victories for Thee this day. I depend on Thee for guidance and help, so be Thou near to me. Take the praise for whatever victories will be won to Thyself. *Amen.*

FEBRUARY 6

Eternal Father:
Thou who art constant yet ever new; Thou who hast created the longing for Thee in me. Thou who alone canst satisfy that longing; I thank Thee. Help me this day to yield my mind, my knowledge and my will to Thee so that Thou canst accomplish in me that which Thou hast purposed. Help me in all things to praise Thy Name. *Amen.*

FEBRUARY 7

Dear Heavenly Father:
I wait upon Thee to direct my path and to order my way. I wait upon Thee to grant me Thy grace to live for Thee. I wait upon Thee to accomplish that which Thou hast purposed. I wait upon Thee to fulfill Thy will in me. Lead me, O Lord, in Thy paths of righteousness, I pray. *Amen.*

FEBRUARY 8

Eternal Father:
Thou art our only Help; Thou art our Keeper and our Guide. Help me to trust Thee in all things, knowing that Thou art able to work everything to Thy good. I thank Thee, Lord, for Thy promise that Thou

wilt never leave us nor forsake us—so keep me near to Thee this day. *Amen.*

FEBRUARY 9

Dear Heavenly Father:
Life becomes more rich and more meaningful the longer I feel Thy Holy Spirit within. I thank Thee for the privilege of knowing Thee, and for being able to call upon Thee and to praise Thee. Dear Lord, Thou art everything to me, and I desire a way to do Thy will. Lead me in the paths of righteousness, and grant me Thy peace. *Amen.*

FEBRUARY 10

Eternal Father:
Thou who makest life accountable; Thou who art the Answer to all of life; I give Thee thanks for the revelation of Thyself in Thy creation, in the gift of Thy Son and in the presence of Thy Holy Spirit within us. It is so sweet to trust Thee, O Lord, and to know that all things come out right with Thee in them. Use me this day, I pray. *Amen.*

FEBRUARY 11

Dear Heavenly Father:
Thou who protecteth us from evil and establisheth joy and peace in our hearts; Thou who art the Source of our strength and the Guide of our life; help me this day to walk in the paths of righteousness and to do Thy will. Receive my thanksgiving for all that Thou art to me. *Amen.*

FEBRUARY 12

Dear Heavenly Father:
To Thee I give most grateful and hearty thanks for all that Thou art to me. Thou hast looked down with mercy upon me, and hast crowned me with

glory and honor. Thou hast touched me with Thine healing hand and I am saved. Use me as Thou wilt, I pray. *Amen.*

FEBRUARY 13

Eternal Father:
Thou who art the Author of all the qualities of goodness, and hast given unto us the ability to choose between good and evil; Thou who art near to help us when we are tempted toward evil; help me this day to remain in the orbit of Thy love so that Thy Holy Spirit will fill me with strength and wisdom, and I will do Thy will. *Amen.*

FEBRUARY 14

Dear Heavenly Father:
Thy ways are past finding out, and Thy mercy is everlasting. Thou who knowest our frame and understandest that we are dust, yet art willing to invest Thine eternal love in us, help me this day to feel Thy presence as I seek to live for Thee. *Amen.*

FEBRUARY 15

Eternal Father:
Thou who providest opportunities to allow me to discover Thy goodness and Thy care; Thou who art always revealing Thy love in different ways; I thank Thee that Thou hast given me another day in which to know Thee better. Guide me and use me, Lord. *Amen.*

FEBRUARY 16

Dear Heavenly Father:
I thank Thee that there is so much for which to give Thee thanks, so much in which we can trust Thee. Thou hast used the simple to confound the great and the foolish to condemn the wise. Thou who

upholdest those who trust in Thee, guide me this day and help me to honor Thee. *Amen.*

FEBRUARY 17

Eternal Father:
For Thine inestimable goodness, I give Thee thanks. Thou who art all wise; Thou who art all love; Thou who hast poured out Thy grace upon us even when we are not worthy. Dear Lord, help me to be ever mindful of Thy goodness and honor Thee in all my living. *Amen.*

FEBRUARY 18

Dear Heavenly Father:
I rejoice in Thee, for I know that Thou art my God and my Savior. Thou knowest me within and without, and Thou carest for me. I yield myself to Thy Holy Spirit, praying that Thou wilt be pleased to work Thy perfect will through me. *Amen.*

FEBRUARY 19

Eternal Father and Our God:
Maker of heaven and earth, Giver of every good and perfect gift, Preserver of those who trust in Thee; Thou whose ways art past finding out, who sendest Thy sun to shine on the just and the unjust; yet Thou who rewardest justice; thank Thee for Thy goodness. Lead me in Thy path this day. *Amen.*

FEBRUARY 20

Dear Heavenly Father:
I thank Thee for the many ways Thou hast provided for me to benefit from Thy goodness. I thank Thee that I can depend upon Thee to work out all things well. Help me, Lord, to trust Thee, for Thou knowest the

end from the beginning, and Thy design and purpose are sure. Help me this day, in all I do, to praise Thee. *Amen.*

FEBRUARY 21

Dear Heavenly Father:
Again I thank Thee for Thy goodness and Thy care, Thou who art my Preserver and my Guide. Thou knowest the way I take, I depend on Thee to walk with me. Help me, O Lord, to be conscious of Thy leading, and grant me the wisdom to do Thy will. Fill me with Thy grace, and do for me even more than I can ask or think. *Amen.*

FEBRUARY 22

Dear Heavenly Father:
As I once more capture a bit of eternity and call upon Thee; as I seek to know Thy will and fulfill Thy purpose for me; as I yield myself to doing Thy bidding; receive me, I pray. Have Thy way, O Lord, and bring to pass that which Thou hast purposed. *Amen.*

FEBRUARY 23

Dear Heavenly Father:
It is only by Thy grace that we are saved, O Lord, and I am thankful that this truth has been revealed to me. I thank Thee that I can claim Thy love and give myself to Thee. Help me to remember that all mankind is in Thy keeping, and Thou desirest our salvation. Use me in accomplishing Thy purpose. *Amen.*

FEBRUARY 24

Dear Heavenly Father:
I thank Thee for Thy constancy, for Thine everlasting love. I thank Thee that Thy mercy is new every morning, and the flow of that mercy is to

usward. Thou who hast thought of us long before we could ever think of ourselves, and hast made provisions for us beyond our knowledge, Lord, I thank Thee. *Amen.*

FEBRUARY 25

Dear Heavenly Father:
Thou in whom I live and move and have my being; Thou who hast ordained my path and ordered my precepts; Thou who art in my beginning and my end; help me to grow in fullness with Thee and direct my life in the way of praise, this day and forever. *Amen.*

FEBRUARY 26

Dear Heavenly Father:
Thou who art from everlasting to everlasting, yet ever new, I thank Thee for this new day, and for Thy goodness and Thy love. I yield anew to Thee my life, my all, that Thou wilt use me in fulfilling Thy purpose for this world. Have Thy way with me, dear Lord, and grant me the knowledge and the wisdom to follow Thee. *Amen.*

FEBRUARY 27

Dear Heavenly Father:
Thou who art the Source of life and all existence, the Giver of every good and perfect gift; Thou who hast given me the privilege of coming to Thee; I thank Thee for the assurance of Thy care. I thank Thee that Thou art with all those who trust Thee and will sustain them forever. *Amen.*

FEBRUARY 28

Dear Heavenly Father:
Thou who art the Source of inspiration and who providest the channels of service, I thank Thee for the privilege of this job. I thank Thee for guidance in leading people. I pray that Thou wilt ever be by my side to remind me of Thy presence. If ever I think that I am doing this alone, just give me a little reminder that Thou art the One who sustains. *Amen.*

FEBRUARY 29

Eternal and Ever-Loving Lord:
I thank Thee for Thy goodness to us. I thank Thee for Thy care. Thou who anticipatest our needs and providest for our wants, and art abundant in Thine offerings, help me this day to be truly grateful for all that Thy bounty supplieth. Lead me in the path of righteousness, I pray. *Amen.*

MARCH

MARCH 1

Dear Heavenly Father:
For a new month and all its blessings, I give Thee thanks. Thou who knowest the end from the beginning, and who preparest that of which we have need, I thank Thee that I am in Thine hand and that Thou carest for me. Help me to honor Thee in my living, and use me to praise Thee. *Amen.*

MARCH 2

Eternal Father:
If only I knew how to thank Thee, I would. Thou who hast done such great things for me, of which I am very glad; Thou who hast given me the privilege of seeing the marvels of Thy creation, and hearing the harmonies of nature, and sensing the comfort of Thy Holy Spirit; I lift my heart in praise of Thee this day. *Amen.*

MARCH 3

Eternal Father:
I realize that this life of mine is a gift from Thee to carry out Thy divine purpose. Thy Spirit beareth witness with my spirit, assuring me that Thou art with me. Grant me the wisdom and the grace to follow Thy leading so that I will accomplish that which Thou hast designed. *Amen.*

MARCH 4

Eternal Father:
Thou who art strong to save, and who hath promised that whosoever cometh unto Thee Thou wilt in no wise cast out, I come to Thee again for refreshment and strength. I come to Thee because I am assured that Thou art willing to lead me and guide me. Use me this day and help me to reflect Thy love, in Jesus' Name. *Amen.*

MARCH 5

Eternal Father:
Thou who art righteous and desirest us to be righteous, I ask Thee to grant me Thy grace. Without Thee and without the knowledge that Thou art near, I am hopeless and bewildered and surely will fail. Breathe Thy Holy Spirit upon me and fill me with life forevermore. Use me in doing Thy will and take the praise to Thyself. *Amen.*

MARCH 6

Dear Heavenly Father:
I thank Thee for Thy mercies poured out upon me and my loved ones, for the constant reminders that Thou art a good God and that Thou art from everlasting to everlasting. Lord, I love Thee and I am grateful to Thee. Help me to continually praise Thee and grant me the skill to share Thy love with others. Use me as Thou wilt, I pray. *Amen.*

MARCH 7

Dear Heavenly Father:
Thou who art my God, my all in all, grant me Thy Holy Spirit that I might walk in the path of truth. Thou who art the Source of all wisdom, and knowest the end from the beginning, help me to live in fullness of Thy purpose and honor Thee. Receive Thou my thanks, I pray. *Amen.*

MARCH 8

Dear Heavenly Father:
Thou in whom there is no east or west, no north or south; Thou who holdest the whole world in Thy hand and in whom all things consist; I thank Thee for the knowledge of Thy love. I thank Thee that Thou

hast promised to be with us even unto the end of the world. Help me to have my mind on Thee in all I do this day. *Amen.*

MARCH 9

Dear Heavenly Father:

I continue to marvel at Thy words. Thou who hast conceived of Thy creation and hast brought us into being; Thou who hath prepared a way whereby we can know Thee; Thou who desirest our love; Lord, I thank Thee. Make me truly worthy of Thee and help me to know and do Thy will. Grant me wisdom, knowledge, and understanding, I pray. *Amen.*

MARCH 10

Dear Heavenly Father:

Thy mystery is beyond our knowing; Thy mercy is beyond our deserving; Thy love is beyond our understanding; Thy peace is beyond our comprehending; so grant us the faith to trust Thee and the joy to praise Thee for all that Thou art, this day and forever. *Amen.*

MARCH 11

Dear Heavenly Father:

I thank Thee that Thy goodness is still extended toward me and I have the privilege of calling Thee Father and coming to thank Thee. Teach me Thy way this day and cause me to fulfill Thy will. Grant me wisdom to follow Thy leading and to be able to discern truth from falsehood. Use me, dear Lord, to do Thy will. *Amen.*

MARCH 12

Dear Heavenly Father:

Thou who hast ordained the world and fixed all things in their places;

Thou who hast established the laws to govern the order of the universe; Thou who hast made mankind to love and worship Thee; I thank Thee that Thou didst include me. I thank Thee for Thy Holy Spirit who witnesseth within me. Guide me this day. *Amen.*

MARCH 13

Dear Heavenly Father:
Thou who hast ordered time, and in Thine own way hast brought me into being; Thou who hast planted the desire of worship within me and satisfiest my longing heart when I come to Thee; Dear Heavenly Father, teach me Thy way and help me to know and do Thy will. Lead me in the paths of righteousness, for Thy Name's sake. *Amen.*

MARCH 14

Eternal Father:
Thou who art always available to answer our call; Thou who grantest comfort to the sad; Thou who offerest strength to the weak; I thank Thee for Thyself and for all that Thou art to me. Help me this day to honor Thee as I live. Please take the praise to Thyself. *Amen.*

MARCH 15

Dear Heavenly Father:
Thou who art the Source of love and who hast established love in the hearts of men, help me this day to love as Thou wouldst have me love so that my fellowmen will know that Thy love floweth within me. Have Thy way with me, O Lord, and let Thy kingdom come and Thy will be done on earth, as it is in Heaven. *Amen.*

MARCH 16

Dear Heavenly Father:

There is excitement and grandeur in knowing that Thou dost direct and control every living thing; that Thou givest strength to the faint, and buildest up the courage of those who are cast down; that Thou art the Source of all goodness. For this I thank Thee. Help me this day to show forth Thy love with understanding. *Amen.*

MARCH 17

Dear Heavenly Father:

I thank Thee that I can rejoice with others who celebrate today. Let peace come among all Thy people everywhere. Dear Lord, establish good will among all mankind, and help us to enjoy the beauty of Thy peace. *Amen.*

MARCH 18

Dear Heavenly Father:

Again I give Thee thanks for granting me the privilege of life and the knowledge of Thy goodness. Thou who art the everlasting Father, the eternal God, the Giver of every good and perfect gift, Thou hast given us Thyself in Jesus Christ. Make me truly worthy of Thee this day. *Amen.*

MARCH 19

Dear Heavenly Father:

Despite the pain I now feel, I am assured that Thou carest. I trust that, in Thine own time, Thou wilt grant relief. I thank Thee that, in all things, I can trust Thee and I can depend upon Thee for help. Bolster my courage this day and help me to feel Thee near. I pledge myself anew to Thee. Help me to honor Thee. *Amen.*

MARCH 20

Dear Heavenly Father:
For the mystery of thought and for the treasures that can be borne on the wings of thought, I thank Thee. Thou hast made it possible for us to be enriched by the flow of Thy love for us, and such love is often manifested in the thoughts which come to us. Fill me this day with those thoughts that will make this world what Thou wilt. *Amen.*

MARCH 21

Eternal Father:
Thy mercy is extended continuously unto us, and Thy truth is ever near to guide us. Help me through Thy Spirit to draw deep from the well of Thine everlasting fountain and be filled with Thy grace. Reveal more of Thy will for me this day, I pray. *Amen.*

MARCH 22

Dear Heavenly Father:
I thank Thee for the newness of Thy love, for the sense of peace that Thine abiding grace affords. I thank Thee, Lord, that Thou hast chosen to be good to me, and I pray that I will follow Thy leading always. I yield myself again to Thee today, praying that Thou wilt be pleased to use me in Thy service. Help me to honor Thee, I pray. *Amen.*

MARCH 23

Dear Heavenly Father:
Thou who art the Source of thought and the Seat of action; Thou who dost stimulate and direct all good deeds; I come again to thank Thee for laying the desire of worship in my being, and for supplying the answer Thyself. Dear Lord, guide me this day to think, speak, and act as Thou wilt have me, and help me to praise Thee. *Amen.*

MARCH 24

Dear Heavenly Father:

Thou who hast established within us the capacity for love, and hast expressed Thy love to us in all Thy creation; Thou who hast fulfilled Thy love in the person of Jesus Christ, who hath declared that whosoever cometh unto Him He will not cast out; be with me today. *Amen.*

MARCH 25

Dear Heavenly Father:

Thou who art a God of mercy and miracle, Thou who hast done for me more than I have asked, Thou who art dependable and trustworthy, Thou who art ever-loving, I thank Thee for all that Thou art, and pledge again myself to serve Thee. Lead me in the path of righteousness this day as I seek to do Thy will. *Amen.*

MARCH 26

Dear Heavenly Father:

Thou who art the Author of communication and hast in time past spoken unto us through the prophets, and in these last days speakest to us through Thy Son Jesus Christ, I thank Thee that Thy Holy Spirit still bears witness that we are Thy children and that, when we call, Thou wilt answer, and when we are yet speaking, Thou wilt hear. *Amen.*

MARCH 27

Eternal Father:

I thank Thee for the joy that Thy love giveth and for the eternal hope that rests in us as we believe in Thee. Make me strong in faith and know assuredly that Thou wilt never leave me nor forsake me. Help me to so dedicate myself to Thee that Thy full purpose is reflected in all I do. *Amen.*

MARCH 28

Eternal Father:
Source of all goodness, Giver of every perfect gift, Thou who hast chosen me, I thank Thee. Lead me, O Lord, to know and to follow Thee. Fill me with Thy grace and let Thy truth ever guide me. I seek only to do Thy will, so order my life to praise Thee. *Amen.*

MARCH 29

Dear Heavenly Father:
Help me to know more of Thy will this day and yield myself to doing Thy bidding. Eternal Lord, Thou who didst conceive us and thought us worthy to be Thy children, make us truly worthy. Cause us to look around and within and realize that it is only by Thy mercy that we are alive. Guide us this day by Thy grace. *Amen.*

MARCH 30

Dear Lord Jesus:
I thank Thee that Thou art the Way, the Truth, the Life; that Thy mercy is everlasting, and that Thy truth endureth to all generations. I thank Thee that Thou art always available to listen to our plea and to answer as we hang our hopes on Thee. I thank Thee, Lord, for the comfort which Thou givest. Help me to abide in Thee. *Amen.*

MARCH 31

Dear Heavenly Father:
Thou who dost use the simple things of this world to confound the wise, and whose mercy endureth from generation to generation, I thank Thee that Thou hast chosen to use me. Grant me wisdom, knowledge, and understanding in doing Thy will. *Amen.*

APRIL

APRIL 1

Dear Heavenly Father:

This is a new day, a new month to us, but to Thee it is all a part of Thine eternity. Thine everlasting grace is mingled in this day before it began and Thine eternal love permeates each moment. I thank Thee, Lord, that all things consist in Thee and that, as we give ourselves to Thee, Thou dost reveal Thyself. Lead me this day, I pray. *Amen.*

APRIL 2

Eternal Father:

Thou who dost communicate through thought, and art ever ready to reveal Thy secrets to us if we would only wait upon Thee; Thou who art the Source of all goodness and all truth, and desirest that humankind should seek Thee and know Thee; lead me this day to a clearer knowledge of Thee as I seek to do Thy will. *Amen.*

APRIL 3

Dear Heavenly Father:

For Thy mercies and protection I thank Thee. Thou hast not dealt with us as we deserve. Thou hast shown us Thy might in the force of the storm, but Thou hast been merciful in protecting us. Lord, Thou art really good to us and I thank Thee. Help me this day to live for Thee and grant me the knowledge to serve Thee aright. *Amen.*

APRIL 4

Eternal Father:

Thou who knowest my frame and understandest that I am dust; Thou who in Thine own wisdom and mercy hast given me the privilege of sharing in Thy marvelous work of creation; Thou who hast planted

Thy Holy Spirit within me, and assurest me that I am a child of Thine; receive my heartfelt thanks and use me in Thy service. *Amen.*

APRIL 5

Eternal Father:
Giver of life, Author of love, Thou within Thine own wisdom hast created the world for Thyself. Thou who hast limited Thyself and hast given us the power to choose and even not to choose Thee, have mercy on our ignorance. Help me this day to praise Thee and to do Thy will. *Amen.*

APRIL 6

Dear Heavenly Father:
It is my privilege to come to Thee and to thank Thee for Thy love and all that Thou art to me and to all the world. Thou who art constant, whose love faileth not, and whose mercy is everlasting, keep me this day in Thy will and guide me in the paths of righteousness. *Amen.*

APRIL 7

Eternal and Ever-Loving God:
I thank Thee that it is my privilege to come to Thee and to claim Thee as Father and Lord. Thou who didst call me into being and hast prospered my way; Thou who knowest my need and providest the satisfaction that fulfills my need; I thank Thee. Help me this day to do Thy will. *Amen.*

APRIL 8

Eternal Father:
Thou who art nearer than breathing and closer than hands and feet, live in me this day and use me in bringing to pass that which Thou hast purposed. I pray for my friends, especially those who do not

acknowledge Thee as their Savior. Help them to know that they are nothing without Thee. *Amen.*

APRIL 9

Eternal Father:

To Thee be the honor and glory. To Thee be the praise and thanks. Thou who hast granted unto me Thy blessings and Thy love; Thou who hast prospered my way; Thou who grantest healing and help; Thou whom I can trust under all circumstances; be with me this day, I pray. *Amen.*

APRIL 10

Dear Heavenly Father:

Thou who knowest all and understandest our weaknesses as well as our strengths, I thank Thee that when we bring them all to Thee Thou art able to sanctify them all and make us worthy of Thee. Help me this day to be mindful of Thine everlasting presence, and of Thine outstretched arm. Help me to rest upon Thee and be sustained by Thee. *Amen.*

APRIL 11

Eternal Father:

Thy mercy is new every morning, and Thy truth endureth to all generations. I feel Thy Holy Spirit within me, and I am drawn to worship Thee. Abide with me, O Lord, and help me to show forth Thy love. Use me as Thou wilt this day, and take the praise to Thyself. *Amen.*

APRIL 12

Eternal Father:

Unto Thee all hearts are open, all desires known. From Thee no secrets are hid. Thou knowest and understandest me afar off, and art acquainted with all my ways. Help me, O Lord, to trust Thee, because from Thee cometh every good and perfect gift. Use me as Thou wilt today. *Amen.*

APRIL 13

Dear Lord Jesus:
Thou who art Savior and Lord; Thou who hast made life meaningful, purposeful, and wonderful; it is so sweet to trust in Thee and to know that Thou art in everything I do. Dear Lord, have Thy way with me this day, and take the praise unto Thyself for all that is accomplished. *Amen.*

APRIL 14

Dear Heavenly Father:
Thou who from the past hast created the present, I thank Thee that Thou hast chosen to have me in it. I trust Thee that as Thou createst the future, Thou wilt continue me in it. Grant me the strength and the wisdom for each day. Help me to consecrate them all to Thee. Live through me, I pray, and let Thy Kingdom come in reality. *Amen.*

APRIL 15

Eternal Father:
I thank Thee that Thou hast revealed Thyself through Thy love. I thank Thee for the example of Jesus Christ, Thy Son. I thank Thee that through Him I have life for evermore. Lead me this day in the path of truth, and grant me wisdom to say and do those things that will honor Thee. *Amen.*

APRIL 16

Dear Heavenly Father:
I thank Thee for the rain and for the greenery of the plants. I thank Thee for Thy blessings of being able to see and appreciate the beauty of

Thy world. I thank Thee most of all for the knowledge that Thou art ever mindful of me. Help me, Lord, to love and serve Thee. Use me as Thou wilt, I pray. *Amen.*

APRIL 17

Dear Heavenly Father:

Thou who hast sent Thy Son Jesus Christ to show us how to live; Thou who didst not spare Him but suffered that he should pay the penalty for my sins; I thank Thee for this matchless gift that makes me free. I give myself to Thee anew that Thou mayest be pleased to use me as Thou wilt. *Amen.*

APRIL 18

Eternal Father:

I claim Thy goodness and Thy promise that there is no good thing that Thou wilt withhold from those who trust Thee. Lord, Thou knowest that I trust Thee for life, for hope, for love. Lead me this day in the paths of righteousness so that I may do Thy will. *Amen.*

APRIL 19

Dear Heavenly Father:

Thou in whom all mystery is revealed because of Thy goodness; Thou who causest all things to work together for good; Thou who canst convert destruction and death to new life and resurrection; I thank Thee. Help me to trust Thee continually and to know that with Thee all will be well. *Amen.*

APRIL 20

Dear Heavenly Father:

Thou on whom I can depend, who art near at all times, and who givest good comfort, help me to feel Thy presence now. Breathe again Thy Holy Spirit within me that I will rejoice in Thee and praise Thy Name. Use me, O Lord, to honor Thee, and cause me always to glorify Thy Name. *Amen.*

APRIL 21

Dear Heavenly Father:
I come to Thee once more only because of Thy goodness and Thy love. I know that Thou art my Keeper and my Guide. I seek to serve Thee with all my heart, soul, mind, and strength. Grant me Thy grace and the wisdom to know and follow Thy will. *Amen.*

APRIL 22

Eternal Father:
Thou who art new every morning; Thou who art ever willing to make Thy way known unto us; declare Thy purpose for me this day. Grant me the wisdom to understand Thy workings. Help me to interpret correctly the plan that Thou reveals. Use me as thou wilt, I pray. *Amen.*

APRIL 23

Eternal Father:
Thou who hast ordained the order of the world, the motions and movements of life; Thou who hast designed each unit of matter and has revealed Thy nature to us; Thou who hast declared Thyself our Father; help me truly to be as a son to Thee. Thank Thee for Thy love, and use me as Thou wilt. *Amen.*

APRIL 24

Dear Heavenly Father:
I thank Thee for Thy past blessings; and because I know that Thou art ever present, and that all of time is caught up in Thee, I thank Thee for all the blessings that are in store for me. Help me to praise Thee continually. Teach me how to love Thee, and give me the right spirit in expressing my gratitude. *Amen.*

APRIL 25

Eternal Father:
I thank Thee for the refreshment gained in rest, for the invigorating energy that cometh from relaxation, and for the joy of knowing that Thou didst make it all possible for me to enjoy. Dear Lord, help me to be ever thankful and to praise Thee always. *Amen.*

APRIL 26

Dear Heavenly Father:
Thou who dost preserve those whom Thou choosest; Thou who dost furnish a table in the wilderness and carest for all Thy creation; I thank Thee that Thou art mindful of me and all my needs. I thank Thee that Thou hast promised never to leave me nor forsake me. Keep me by Thy grace this day. *Amen.*

APRIL 27

Eternal Father:
Thou who art our Strength; Thou who art the Source of life; Thou who art always willing to fill us with Thy Holy Spirit and speed us on our way; I thank Thee for Thyself and for the comfort of Thy presence. It is good to be with Thee, O Lord, and I pray that I will do Thy bidding this day. *Amen.*

APRIL 28

Eternal Father:

That Thou hast granted me the joy of knowing Thee, and the privilege of claiming Thee as Savior and Lord; that Thou hast made my path clear and hast directed my way; I praise Thee and pledge to Thee my all. Use me this day as Thou wilt. In Thy Name, I pray. *Amen.*

APRIL 29

Dear Heavenly Father:

For the realization of Thy love, and the understanding of Thy promises, I thank Thee, Lord. For the opportunities to serve Thee, and for the privilege of being chosen by Thee, I thank Thee, Lord. For the constant assurance of Thine abiding presence and for the sustaining power of Thy Word, I thank Thee, Lord. *Amen.*

APRIL 30

Dear Heavenly Father:

Thou who hast planted potential in us and hast given us the possibility of becoming all we are capable of being; Thou who art with us to sustain us and allow us to achieve even beyond our own imaginings; be with me this day and help me to accomplish that which is possible. *Amen.*

May

MAY 1

Dear Heavenly Father:

For Thy many blessings I give Thee thanks this day. Thy mercy is everlasting, and Thy truth endureth to all generations. Thou hast made known anew Thy goodness, and I am grateful. Lead me this day in the paths of righteousness. Help me to show forth Thy love so that others will know Thy goodness and worship Thee in spirit and in truth. *Amen.*

MAY 2

Eternal and Ever-Loving Lord:

Thou who hast given us Thyself; Thou who hast limited Thyself for our sake so that we can be drawn to Thee; I thank Thee for Thy goodness; I thank Thee for Thy care; I thank Thee for Thine everlasting presence within and around me. Use me this day as Thou wilt. *Amen.*

MAY 3

Dear Heavenly Father:

I realize that humility is the consciousness of dependence on Thy divine grace. I know that without Thy goodness and forgiveness none of us could live. So, dear Lord, I thank Thee for Thine everlasting love, and for Thy continued grace toward me. Help me to do Thy will this day. *Amen.*

MAY 4

Eternal Father:

Thou who hast granted us the revelation of Thyself in the Person of Jesus Christ; Thou who hast made plain to us that Thou art our Father and that, as a Father pitieth his children, so Thou pitieth those who call upon Thee; have mercy upon me this day and help me to do Thy will. *Amen.*

MAY 5

Dear Heavenly Father:
I thank Thee for being with me to guide me and remind me that I am Thine. Without Thee, Lord, I am nothing. I need to feel Thee ever within, for then I know that I will be kept in the paths of righteousness. Lead and direct me this day and help me in all my doing to honor Thine Holy Name. *Amen.*

MAY 6

Dear Heavenly Father:
This is a new morning to me, O Lord, but to Thee it is eternally with Thee. I ask Thee for wisdom, knowledge, and understanding in fulfilling the demands of this day. Help me to be an instrument of Thine, doing that which Thou desirest. Take the praise unto Thyself when I please Thee. *Amen.*

MAY 7

Dear Lord and Father:
Thou who hast made us for Thyself; Thou who desirest to have fellowship with us; Thou who hast planted within us the sense of worship; I come to Thee this day pledging again my loyalty, offering my will, praying that Thou wilt help me to know how to truly worship Thee. Guide me this day, I pray. *Amen.*

MAY 8

Dear Heavenly Father:
Giver of every good and perfect gift and Orderer of our given course, I thank Thee this day for the satisfaction of coming to Thee and claiming Thy promise. Thou who knowest the end from the beginning and art able to guide me into the paths of truth, lead me today to fulfill Thy will. Grant me Thy grace, O Lord, to honor Thee in what I do. *Amen.*

MAY 9

Dear Heavenly Father:
I thank Thee for life and for the privilege of enjoying it. If this life is so great, O Lord, how much more will life everlasting be? Thou who art in this life and hast promised to be with us forever, grant me the knowledge, the grace and the will to live for Thee. *Amen.*

MAY 10

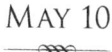

Eternal and Most Ever-Loving God:
I come to Thee once more to thank Thee for Thy goodness and Thy care. I thank Thee for Thine everlasting promises, which extend from generation to generation. I thank Thee for Thy mercy, which is new every morning. Lead me, I pray, in the paths of righteousness for Thine own Name's sake. *Amen.*

MAY 11

Dear Heavenly Father:
Thou who hast taken responsibility for our creation and hast provided for all our needs; Thou who hast made us for Thyself, and desirest that we know Thee and give ourselves to Thee; I thank Thee that it is my privilege to claim Thee as Father and I pray that Thou wilt help me to do Thy will. *Amen.*

MAY 12

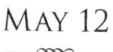

Dear Heavenly Father:
For the lesson of faith, I give Thee thanks. Thou who hast sustained Thy children through the ages, and hast given them the will to trust Thee; Thou who hast promised and proven that when we trust Thee Thou art faithful to Thy promise; I trust Thee even now and depend on Thee. *Amen.*

MAY 13

Dear Heavenly Father:
Thou who hast given us Thyself and all the power to become Thy children; Thou whose mercy is everlasting, and whose truth endureth to all generations; Thy compassion faileth not, and Thou art always willing and ready to reveal more of Thy love to us. Live through me this day, I pray. *Amen.*

MAY 14

Dear Heavenly Father:
Thou who art working Thy purpose out as day succeeds to day; Thou who hast brought me into Thy plan and hast prepared the way wherein I walk; I thank Thee for Thy goodness and Thy care. I thank Thee that Thou knowest the way that I take and will walk with me. Use me as Thou wilt this day. *Amen.*

MAY 15

Eternal Father:
Thou who lovest us even more than we could ever love ourselves; Thou who knowest our need more than we could ever realize; Thou who art the Sustainer and Preserver of all who trust in Thee; guide me today and help me to do Thy will. *Amen.*

MAY 16

Dear Heavenly Father:
Thou who art great and causest those who trust in Thee to do great things, I thank Thee for Thy love. I thank Thee that I can trust Thee. Grant me wisdom to live the life that pleases Thee. Be with me every minute of every day. Help me always to rejoice in Thee. *Amen.*

MAY 17

Eternal Father:
I thank Thee that all Thy creation is special and unique, and that Thy source is so rich that all Thy thoughts are new. I know that with this new day hath come new love, so help me to rejoice in Thee and claim Thy goodness and Thy care. Help me to fulfill Thy plan and to praise Thine Holy Name. *Amen.*

MAY 18

Dear Heavenly Father:
To Thee I come for grace and for wisdom to know how best to represent Thee. I know that Thy purpose for me is to do Thy will, but I desire to be led by Thee in the paths of righteousness and service. Help me to follow Thee, O Lord, and to yield myself fully to Thee this day. *Amen.*

MAY 19

Dear Heavenly Father:
Thou who carest for me even more than I could ever think of caring for myself; Thou who hast thought of and providest for my well-being; I give Thee most hearty thanks for all Thy goodness toward me. Help me to rejoice in Thee this day and forever. *Amen.*

MAY 20

Dear Heavenly Father:
Thou who openest new opportunities in which I can see Thy goodness; Thou who speakest in so many languages and in so many ways; grant me the wisdom to know when Thou art speaking to me directly. Grant me the grace to follow as Thou leadest. Grant me love to share with all. *Amen.*

MAY 21

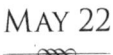

Eternal Father:
Thou who hast chosen to include me in Thy plan for the world, and who hast done such wondrous things for me, I thank Thee. Grant me the wisdom, the knowledge, and the understanding that I need under all circumstances, so that I can accomplish that which Thou desirest. *Amen.*

MAY 22

Dear Heavenly Father:
All that we are comes from Thee. Thou art the Source of our being. I come once more to thank Thee for the knowledge of Thee and for the desire to serve and adore Thee. My heart is joyous with the knowledge that Thou carest for me and welcomest my worship. Lead me this day in the path of righteousness and help me to honor Thee. *Amen.*

MAY 23

Eternal Father:
Thou who art abundant in Thy grace and art everlasting in Thy love; Thou who hast promised to draw near to those who draw near to Thee; I come once more to thank Thee for Thyself and to ask that Thou wilt keep me near Thee. Help me to do Thy will this day. *Amen.*

MAY 24

Dear Lord and Father of Mankind:
I thank Thee that Thou hast made it possible for us to have fellowship with Thee. Our hearts are restless until we find Thee. Thou givest peace. Grow, Thou, in me, O Lord, until every part of me glows with Thy fire divine, and help me to honor Thee in all I do. Use me this day as Thou wilt. *Amen.*

MAY 25

Dear Heavenly Father:
Thou who art eternal and who hath our time in Thy grasp; Thou who hast loaned us this brief moment to enjoy the glory of Thy creation and prepare ourselves for Thine everlasting habitation; help me to give myself fully to Thee that Thou wilt truly have Thy way with me. Prepare me for Thy service, I pray this day. *Amen.*

MAY 26

Dear Heavenly Father:
Thou who art infinite and comprehendest all the workings of the world; Thou who understandest my thoughts afar off and art acquainted with all my ways; help me to trust Thee and to know that Thou doest all things well. Use me and mine this day to do Thy will. *Amen.*

MAY 27

Dear Heavenly Father:
Breathe Thy Holy Spirit upon me again that I may go forward in Thy grace. Grant me wisdom that I may choose the right path. Give me strength to tackle that which seems difficult. Help me to remember that Thou hast promised to be with me always, even unto the end of the world. *Amen.*

MAY 28

Dear Heavenly Father:
Thou who didst pour Thy Holy Spirit upon the Disciples in the upper room, and promised Thy people that Thou wilt never leave us nor forsake us, help me to feel Thee near me this day, and grant me wisdom to do Thy will. *Amen.*

MAY 29

Our Father God:
Thou in Thy wisdom hast made the world and hast brought us into being. Thou who hast ordered our path and prepared our end, I thank Thee that Thou art in control and that we cannot take one step without Thine aid. Dear Lord, the longer we stay with Thee, the safer we are. Help me to abide in Thee this day and fill me with Thy Holy Spirit. *Amen.*

MAY 30

Dear Heavenly Father:
Thou in whom all things consist; Thou who knowest the end from the beginning, and hast ordered our path; I thank Thee that Thou hast revealed Thyself through Thy Son Jesus Christ, who hast sent the Holy Spirit to comfort and preserve us. Be Thou with me this day, I pray. *Amen.*

MAY 31

Dear Heavenly Father:
Thou who art Truth and desirest us to be truthful; Thou who art Love and desirest us to be loving; Thou who art Grace and desirest us to be gracious; help me this day to live out these qualities of Thyself with which Thou hast blessed me. Guide me, O Lord, and use me as Thou wilt. *Amen.*

JUNE

JUNE 1

Dear Heavenly Father:
Thou who settlest me and assurest me that all my ways are known by Thee; Thou who carest for me even more than I can care for myself; Thou who hast charted my course and hast promised to be with me all the way; Lord, I thank Thee. Help me always to feel Thee near me and guide me in the path of Thy truth. *Amen.*

JUNE 2

Dear Heavenly Father:
I thank Thee for putting within me the desire to do good. Give me the grace and the wisdom and the strength to fulfill Thy will. Dear Lord, if Thou desirest sacrifice, I would give it; but all that Thou desirest is my love, so I yield my all to Thee. Use me as Thou wilt. *Amen.*

JUNE 3

Eternal Father:
Teach me to number my days so that I may apply my heart unto Thy wisdom. Teach me to know Thy full purpose for my life, and grant me the will and the knowledge to fulfill it. Teach me to rejoice in Thee, knowing that Thou wilt bring to pass that which Thou hast purposed. Guide me this day, I pray. *Amen.*

JUNE 4

Dear Heavenly Father:
Thou who art Mystery, yet so clear in the way Thou manifest Thy love; Thou who art in the beginning and at the same time in the end of every day; Thou who guidest the lives of those who put their trust in Thee; be with me this day and help me to feel Thee near. Grant me the grace to do Thy divine will, I pray. *Amen.*

JUNE 5

Eternal and Ever-Loving God:
Thou who hast created us for Thyself to do Thy will and accomplish that which Thou hast ordered, I thank Thee, Lord, for the knowledge of Thee and for the desire to follow Thee. I thank Thee that Thy sources are greater than I can imagine, and yet all Thy resources are available to me. Help me to abide in Thee and do Thy will this day. *Amen.*

JUNE 6

Dear Heavenly Father:
I thank Thee that in all things I can trust Thee. I thank Thee that Thou understandest my inward desires. Help me, Lord, to follow Thy leadings and do Thy divine will. Give me the wisdom to know the difference between my desire and Thy will. Use me this day, I pray. *Amen.*

JUNE 7

Eternal Father:
Thou who callest us as we are, and art able to use us with what we have; Thou who desirest a humble and a contrite heart, and will not despise those who are penitent; I thank Thee, dear Lord, that Thou hast made a way whereby we might approach Thee and know that we are redeemed by Thy love. *Amen.*

JUNE 8

Dear Heavenly Father:
I cannot find how to say it differently, and even if I did, it would still mean that I thank Thee for Thy goodness and Thy love. I thank Thee that Thou art always available to hear and answer prayer. I thank Thee,

Lord, that when I come to Thee, I know that Thou carest. Lead me, I pray. *Amen.*

JUNE 9

Dear Heavenly Father:
Thou who art the Father of all and carest for each of us alike; Thou who art mindful of us even more than we can be of ourselves; Lord, I thank Thee for Thy goodness and Thy love. Lead me this day in the paths of righteousness and grant me wisdom to do Thy will. *Amen.*

JUNE 10

Dear Heavenly Father:
For the love that is poured out upon me again, I thank Thee. For the promise that is real to me this day, I give Thee thanks. For the goodness of which I am not even aware, I praise Thy Name. Make me worthy to be Thy child, and give me the grace to live for Thee this day. *Amen.*

JUNE 11

Dear Heavenly Father:
I thank Thee for Thy constant guidance and instruction through Thy Holy Spirit, and through Thy Word. I thank Thee that no matter what the situation, I can depend upon Thy leading. Grant me wisdom continually to follow Thee, and take the praise for the work Thou dost accomplish in me. *Amen.*

JUNE 12

Our Father God:
Giver of life, Giver of hope, Preserver of mankind, Prosperer of our way; Lord, I thank Thee that Thy ways are past finding out, but that Thy love is everlasting and is ever present with us. Thou to whom we

can come at all times and tell all our secrets; Thou who art ever ready to listen to our plea; guide me today, O Lord, and help me to honor Thee. *Amen.*

JUNE 13

Dear Heavenly Father:
I thank Thee for Thine everlasting goodness and Thy care. Thou who hast chosen to bring me into being and prosper my way with all Thy mercies; Thou who hast made me to realize Thy love; help me to give myself fully to Thee that Thou canst use me in Thy service. *Amen.*

JUNE 14

Dear Heavenly Father:
Thou art the Source of hope; even when the world seems to be coming in on us, we can still trust in Thee with an assurance that Thou wilt save us. I thank Thee for the manifestation of Thy saving power in the past, and for Thy promise in the future. Help me to love Thee, Lord. *Amen.*

JUNE 15

Dear Heavenly Father:
So perfect Thou art that all Thy handiwork proclaims Thee. For the privilege of enjoying Thy creation, I thank Thee. For the joy of benefiting from Thy mercy, I adore Thee. For the hope of salvation and the gift of everlasting life in Thee, I depend on Thee. Use me this day as Thou wilt, I pray. *Amen.*

JUNE 16

Dear Heavenly Father:
I thank Thee that Thou hast established hope in us, that Thou hast convinced us that all things work together for good with those who love Thee. Teach me to trust Thee, and to always remember that Thou art

in charge. Help me to praise and rejoice in Thee this day and forever. *Amen.*

JUNE 17

Dear Heavenly Father:
Unto Thee, O Lord, do I lift up my voice. Unto Thee do I offer my praise. Thou who hast sought me long before I was aware of Thee; Thou who art thoughtful of me when I am not thinking of Thee; I thank Thee for Thy goodness and Thy love, and I pray that Thy Holy Spirit will guide me this day. *Amen.*

JUNE 18

Dear Heavenly Father:
By Thy will I have come to plant another seed. By Thy mercy it will be watered and fed. By Thy love may it grow and bear, that the hungry may gather food from it, and the weary may find rest by it, that the birds of the air may make their nest in it. Dear Lord, prosper the work of Thy servant. *Amen.*

JUNE 19

Dear Heavenly Father:
I thank Thee that Thou art Mystery and uncomprehendable, yet through Thy love Thou art knowable. Thou carest for all who come to Thee. Thou answerest prayers of all who call upon Thee. I come once more to praise Thee for whom Thou art, and ask that Thou wilt keep me in Thy way. *Amen.*

JUNE 20

Eternal Father:
Unto whom all hearts are open and all desires known; from whom no

secrets are hidden; I thank Thee that Thou understandest the desires within me, yet Thou knowest and directest the order of that which is best for me. Grant me the wisdom to accept Thy will. *Amen.*

JUNE 21

Dear Heavenly Father:
It is so easy for us to forget Thee; yet Thou art always mindful of us and art always providing for our well-being. Thou who hast prepared the good things for not only this life but for when Thou callest us to abide eternally with Thee, I thank Thee. *Amen.*

JUNE 22

Eternal Father:
I thank Thee for the progress in my work, for Thy guiding hand and Thine everlasting love. I thank Thee for the ability to think and plan and to see things take meaningful form. Thou, who art the Author of all creative force, lead me, Lord, to fulfill Thy design this day. *Amen.*

JUNE 23

Dear Heavenly Father:
I thank Thee for Thy goodness manifested in the world. I can see Thy purposive will being fulfilled. Thou who desirest us to yield ourselves to Thee so Thou canst work Thy divine will in us and have Thy kingdom come on earth as it is in heaven, help me this day, Lord, to so follow Thy leading that I will help a little more toward the fulfillment of Thy will. *Amen.*

JUNE 24

Dear Heavenly Father:
Thy will be done in me as Thou desirest. Grant me the grace to yield to

Thee. Lead me, O Lord, in the paths of righteousness, and help me to serve Thee aright. I am honored that Thou didst choose me. Help me always to know that Thy promise to be with me is real. Help me this day to honor Thee. *Amen.*

JUNE 25

Dear Heavenly Father:

For journeying mercies, I thank Thee, Lord. For the assurance that Thou art with me wherever I go and how ever I travel, I thank Thee, Lord. I am conscious that underneath are Thine everlasting arms. Help me always to rely on Thee and do Thy will. *Amen.*

JUNE 26

Dear Heavenly Father:

Thou who sendest inspiration and support through Thy Word, and guardest us by Thy Spirit, I thank Thee that Thou art dependable. Thou guardest through the rough and the smooth, and art ever near to sustain. Be Thou near me this day, O Lord, and help me to feel Thy presence. *Amen.*

JUNE 27

Dear Heavenly Father:

Thy love is everlasting, and Thy truth endureth to all generations. Help me this day to speak Thy truth and to bring comfort to those who are sad. Help me to love so that others will know Thy love. Help me to work that Thy will be done. *Amen.*

JUNE 28

Dear Heavenly Father:
I thank Thee for the leading of Thy Holy Spirit, who infuses good thoughts within me. I thank Thee that I can depend on Thee to see me through in all circumstances. Help me this day to trust Thee. Help me to do just what Thou wilt have me to do. Manifest Thy will in my living, I pray. *Amen.*

JUNE 29

Dear Heavenly Father:
Thou who hast done more for me than I can either imagine or name; Thou who art more mindful of me than I can be of myself; I thank Thee for the evidence of Thy mercies, and ask that Thou wilt keep me close to Thee. Help me always to choose the best above the better, and guide me in fulfilling Thy will. *Amen.*

JUNE 30

Eternal Father and My God:
Thou who art our only defense, our only help, our only way; Thou who hast placed us in this world to know Thee as Creator, Redeemer, and Lord; I thank Thee that Thy truth has been revealed to me. Help me this day to live in Thee. *Amen.*

JULY

JULY 1

Dear Heavenly Father:

I thank Thee for a new day and a new month. Thou who hast been my dwelling place throughout, I depend on Thee for the future. Help me, dear Lord, to honor Thee in all I do and grant me Thy grace to know Thy will. I am Thine, dear Lord, so keep me in Thy way, I pray. *Amen.*

JULY 2

Dear Heavenly Father:

I thank Thee, Lord, for the privilege of life and for all Thy mercies. I thank Thee for faith in Thee and for the comfort that Thou providest. I rejoice in Thee because I have evidence that Thou carest for me. Help me, Lord, to serve Thee with all my being. Guide me this day, I pray. *Amen.*

JULY 3

Dear Heavenly Father:

Thou who knowest what is good for me, and providest it; Thou who hast my interest at heart and hast promised never to leave me nor forsake me; I thank Thee for Thy love. I thank Thee that I can depend upon Thee to lead me into the paths of truth. Help me at all times to rely upon Thee. Grant me the grace to know and to do Thy will. *Amen.*

JULY 4

Eternal Father:

I thank Thee that Thou art always near to grant comfort and guidance. Thou art always ready to lead in the path of truth. Help me, O Lord, to feel Thy presence near and to go forth with the assurance that I am doing Thy will. Fulfill Thy purpose in me this day. *Amen.*

JULY 5

Dear Lord Jesus:
I thank Thee for all that Thou art, for revealing the heart of the Father to us, and for promising that Thou wilt never leave us nor forsake us. All that Thou desirest is that we accept Thee as Lord and Savior, and Thou workest Thy purpose through us. Be Thou with me this day, I pray. *Amen.*

JULY 6

Dear Heavenly Father:
I thank Thee that Thou art still with us and carest for us. Thy love is new every morning. Thou who already knowest what the end of this day is, help me through it and guide me in it that I may honor Thee every moment of it. Help me to rejoice in Thee and draw me closer every minute. *Amen.*

JULY 7

Dear Heavenly Father:
I come to Thee for wisdom, Thou who art the Source, Thou who art the Way. Guide me this day with Thy Holy Spirit, so that I will be able to think, speak, and act according to Thy truth. Use me to advance Thy Kingdom here on earth, I pray in Thy Name. *Amen.*

JULY 8

Dear Heavenly Father:
With this new day, I claim Thy renewed blessing, Thine everlasting love, and Thine eternal peace. Thou who coverest me with Thy grace and shelterest me with Thy goodness, receive my thanks, I pray, and help me in all things to praise Thy Name. *Amen.*

JULY 9

Dear Heavenly Father:

I thank Thee for the revelation of Thy Fatherhood and for the gift of Thy Son Jesus Christ. I thank Thee for the benefit of salvation to all who acknowledge Thee. I thank Thee that Thy truth endureth to all generations. Help me this day to grow closer to Thee. In all my doing, help me to honor Thee, I pray. *Amen.*

JULY 10

Dear Heavenly Father:

I thank Thee for Thy goodness, I thank Thee for Thy love, I thank Thee that Thou didst consider to bring me into being and to give me the joy of knowing Thee. Help me, O Lord, in all things to honor Thee and use me according to Thy will. *Amen.*

JULY 11

Dear Heavenly Father:

Thou who hast ordered my life and hast filled it with activity; Thou who hast called me to serve in ways that Thou hast chosen; lead me, O Lord, to abide in Thee so that all I do will be blessed by Thee. Fill my life with praise and use me as Thou wilt. *Amen.*

JULY 12

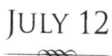

Dear Heavenly Father:

Thou who knowest all things, yet accommodates our limitations; Thou who art so good, yet accepteth us even with our failings; Thou who lovest at all times, yet accepteth us who oftentimes hate; I thank Thee for all that Thou art, and pledge myself again to serve and do Thy will. *Amen.*

JULY 13

Dear Heavenly Father:
I thank Thee for life and all the possibilities of it. I thank Thee that Thou considerest me all along the way. I thank Thee that Thine everlasting presence surroundest me from day to day, and that Thou keepest my going out and my coming in. Help me always to honor Thee, I pray. *Amen.*

JULY 14

Dear Heavenly Father:
Thou to whom I owe all that I am and will be; Thou who hast charted my course and kept me by Thy grace; Thou who continues to sustain me and grant me peace; use me this day and help me to praise Thy Name. *Amen.*

JULY 15

Dear Heavenly Father:
I thank Thee that Thou art righteousness and that, as we put our trust in Thee and walk in Thy way, we are brought to appreciate the fullness of Thy truth. I thank Thee that I can trust Thee to work out Thy purpose in me, and once more I give myelf, that Thou wilt be pleased to do Thy will in me. *Amen.*

JULY 16

Dear Heavenly Father:
For a clearer realization of Thy love and for the lessons of faith which Thou hast given, I give Thee thanks. Build me up to truly understand Thy workings and strengthen my faith in Thee. Thou who desirest my all, and art willing to make me whole, use me as Thou wilt, I pray. *Amen.*

JULY 17

Dear Heavenly Father:

I thank Thee for the privilege of life and for all the benefits with which it comes. Thou who hast ordered my being and set forth its course, Thou art ever near to guide and sustain. Help me ever to acknowledge Thy goodness and always do Thy will. Lead me this day in Thy service, I pray. *Amen.*

JULY 18

Dear Heavenly Father:

Help me to be constant in loving and serving Thee. My heart is fixed upon doing Thy will and seeking after that which will please Thee. Let Thy Holy Spirit guide me as I endeavor to do Thy will. Use me always, I pray *Amen.*

JULY 19

Dear Heavenly Father:

Thou who art the Source of life and the Orderer of my way; Thou who hast designed all I might do for Thee today; help me to feel Thy presence within and cause me to show forth Thy love throughout, that those who see my work may glorify Thee. *Amen.*

JULY 20

Dear Heavenly Father:

Thou who knowest my down sitting and my uprising, who understandest my thoughts afar off and art acquainted with all my ways; Thou to whom I really cannot tell anything new, yet I feel fulfilled when I come to Thee. I find clarity when I state my case to Thee, and am comforted by Thee. Hear my prayer for strength this day, O Lord, and help me to do Thy will. *Amen.*

JULY 21

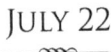

Dear Heavenly Father:
Thou who fashionest all creatures after their kind and givest themes of praise to all Thy creation, I come once more to honor Thee for Thy creativity. I thank Thee that Thou art doing all things well and that, as we place our lives in Thy hand, we find ourselves becoming even beyond our own expectations. *Amen.*

JULY 22

Eternal Father:
Thou who allowest me to write upon the pages of each day those words, those acts, those desires which I dedicate to Thee, I come again to write anew and to pledge once more that my deepest hope is to do Thy will. Grant me the wisdom to know Thy will, and provide me with the strength to do it. Help me when I am through to know that I have only done my duty. *Amen.*

JULY 23

Dear Heavenly Father:
Thou who art the Source of all wisdom, I come to Thee again for instruction, guidance, and leading. I need Thee every minute of every day, and depend upon Thy grace to sustain me. Thou who knowest all the challenges of this day, help me to meet each in Thy Spirit. Use me as Thou wilt, I pray. *Amen.*

JULY 24

Dear Heavenly Father:
Thou who art Father of all and who understandest all my needs; Thou who hast provided for me in the past and art still pouring out Thy

blessings upon me; help me to trust Thee for the future, knowing that Thou art already there. Receive my thanksgiving, I pray, this day. *Amen.*

JULY 25

Dear Heavenly Father:

It is only by Thy grace that we are saved. I am conscious of Thy goodness, O Lord, and of Thy tender mercies. Help me to abide in Thee, that the steam of life that flows from Thee will constantly refresh me and give me strength to do Thy divine will. *Amen.*

JULY 26

Dear Heavenly Father:

Thou who keepest secrets and knowest all about us yet carest for us all, I thank Thee that unto Thee all hearts are open and to Thee all desires are known. Thou who knowest my future and hast already planned those good things for me, help me to trust Thee and live for Thee each day. *Amen.*

JULY 27

Dear Heavenly Father:

I thank Thee for all that Thou art, for all that Thou shall be, and for Thine eternal promise that Thou wilt be with me unto the end of the age. Dear Lord, Thou offerest comfort and hope. Thou grantest security and confidence. Thy mercy is everlasting, and I am grateful to Thee. *Amen.*

JULY 28

Dear Heavenly Father:

Thou whose mercy is everlasting and whose truth endureth to all generations, I thank Thee. I thank Thee that Thou art available to me and that Thy Holy Spirit witnesseth with my spirit, assuring me that I am Thine. Help me to feel Thee near me this day and help me to live for Thee in all that I do. *Amen.*

JULY 29

Dear Heavenly Father:
Thou who hast established me and hast given me the opportunities and privileges that come to me day by day, I thank Thee, Lord. As I learn more about Thy love, not only for me but for everyone in the world, help me, I pray, to translate the knowledge into language that others may know Thee more. *Amen.*

JULY 30

Dear Heavenly Father:
Thou who hast provided forgiveness for us and hast taught us to forgive those who trespass against us, give me the forgiving spirit that I will remember what Thou hast done for me so that I, too, will forgive others. Lead me this day in the paths of righteousness for Thy Name's sake. *Amen.*

JULY 31

Dear Heavenly Father:
I come to Thee for guidance and ask that Thou wilt show me the way. Help me not to take one step without Thine aid. Fulfill Thy will within Thine own time and help me to praise Thee continually. Thou art so good to me and I find such sweet satisfaction in trusting Thee. Live through me, I pray. *Amen.*

AUGUST

AUGUST 1

Dear Heavenly Father:

I thank Thee, dear Lord, for Thy marvelous works upon me. Thou leadest me in the paths of righteousness and makest my heart to rejoice in Thy goodness. I thank Thee that Thou art so dependable and that Thy mercy is so everlasting. Keep me close to Thee, I pray. *Amen.*

AUGUST 2

Dear Heavenly Father:

I thank Thee that Thou hast revealed Thyself to me through Thy Son Jesus Christ, my Savior. I thank Thee for Thy promises preserved through Thy Word and administered by Thy Holy Spirit. I rejoice in Thy goodness and glory in Thy love. Use me this day to honor Thee, I pray. *Amen.*

AUGUST 3

Dear Heavenly Father:

For all Thy goodness and Thy mercy I give Thee thanks. Thou who hast been more mindful of me than I would be of myself; Thou who hast provided all that I have needed and hast promised to continue providing all that I shall need; I thank and praise Thee. Help me in my living to always thank Thee. *Amen.*

AUGUST 4

Dear Heavenly Father:

Thou who art the Fount of every blessing, the Source of all goodness, I thank Thee for the privilege of knowing that Thou carest and providest for all my needs. Keep me close to Thee this day, and help me in my living to praise Thy Name. *Amen.*

AUGUST 5

Dear Heavenly Father:
Thou who art high over all and art crowned with majesty and grace; Thou who hast made Thyself known to us through Thy Son Jesus Christ; Thou who declarest that whosoever cometh unto Thee, Thou wilt in no wise cast out; I come to Thee today to thank Thee for all Thou art. *Amen.*

AUGUST 6

Dear Heavenly Father:
To come to Thee again gives me joy. To praise Thy Name gives me peace. To honor Thee makes me know the source of my being. Receive my thanks once more for all that Thou art to me. Thou givest me all the reason in the world to live and to love. Use me this day to do Thy will, I pray. *Amen.*

AUGUST 7

Dear Heavenly Father:
Thou who art the Source of our being and pourest out Thy loving kindness and tender mercies toward me; I thank Thee for another privilege of coming to Thee. Through Thy Holy Spirit, reveal Thy will to me this day and grant me the wisdom to fulfill Thy desire. Hear my prayer, I ask in Thy Name. *Amen.*

AUGUST 8

Dear Heavenly Father:
For another good day I give Thee thanks. For Thy grace which is extended and Thy promise which is steadfast, I praise Thy Name. Help me to be ever-mindful of Thee and grant me the wisdom to know Thy will. Use me, O Lord, to show forth Thy love, and grant me Thy peace. *Amen.*

August 9

Dear Heavenly Father:

Thou hast given me reason to thank Thee for Thy protection. Thou hast kept me from tragedy and misfortune. I thank Thee that Thou hast been my Keeper. Have mercy upon those who suffer, Lord, and direct my efforts to bring them comfort. *Amen.*

August 10

Dear Heavenly Father:

Thou who art the Source of my faith, the hope of my life, Thou knowest and carest for me. Help me, Lord, to trust Thee and give me the faith to know that all things work together for good with those who trust Thee. Guide me this day and help me to do Thy will. *Amen.*

August 11

Dear Heavenly Father:

Thou in whom we live and move and have our being; Thou who hast chosen us for Thyself; grant me this day the wisdom to serve Thee aright. Help me to show forth Thy goodness and Thy love. Help me that, as I live, others will know assuredly that Thy Spirit guidest me. Use me this day, I pray. *Amen.*

August 12

Dear Heavenly Father:

To Thee be the glory, the praise, the honor for Thy keeping care and tender mercies. That Thou art constant, forever loving, forever forgiving, Thou on whom we can depend to do miracles as Thou choosest. Lord, I thank Thee that Thou knowest all things and that nothing is hidden from Thee. Help me to abide in Thee this day. *Amen.*

AUGUST 13

Dear Heavenly Father:

Thou who openest up the stream of love, knowledge, and wisdom to those whom Thou choosest; Thou who dost select Thy people for various tasks; I pledge myself again this day to Thy will and ask that Thou wilt be pleased to use me. Help me to follow Thee and accomplish that which Thou desirest. *Amen.*

AUGUST 14

Dear Heavenly Father:

Grant me the strength, the knowledge, and the wisdom for this day. Help me to feel Thy presence with me, and allow me to operate under the guidance of Thy Holy Spirit. I need Thee every minute of the day, so help me to do that which I must with Thy hand upon me. I depend upon Thee, Lord. *Amen.*

AUGUST 15

Dear Heavenly Father:

Thou who art love and hast given us Thyself; Thou who hast revealed Thyself in Thy Son Jesus Christ, who is our example and our hope; I thank Thee, Lord, for this special gift and for the knowledge that whosoever receives Jesus is saved forever. Thank Thee for this privilege. *Amen.*

AUGUST 16

Dear Heavenly Father:

I thank Thee that I can trust Thee in all things, Thou who knowest everything and who hast promised to keep that which we commit unto Thee. Dear Lord, Thou hast done for me more than I can ask or think.

I thank Thee. I lay myself again in Thy hand, with the assurance that Thou wilt have Thy way. *Amen.*

AUGUST 17

Dear Heavenly Father:

Thou who art everlasting and whose love endureth forever, help me in coming to Thee not to consider it routine, but to know that new every morning is Thy love. Fill me with that freshness and zeal that greet every day with a new opportunity to serve Thee. Use me this day, I pray. *Amen.*

AUGUST 18

Dear Heavenly Father:

I thank Thee that, from the abundance of Thy mercy, Thou hast again poured out a blessing. Help me to use to the full the gifts Thou hast given me to honor and glorify Thy Name. Eternal Father, guide my path and help me not to take one step without Thine aid. Use me fully in Thy service, I pray. *Amen.*

AUGUST 19

Dear Heavenly Father:

Thou knowest my frame and understandest that I am dust, yet Thou hast chosen to love me and choosest me to do Thy work. Thou hast blessed me with the knowledge that Thou art a loving Father who showerest all Thy children with Thy mercy. Again this day I yield myself to Thee. Use me as Thou wilt, I pray. *Amen.*

AUGUST 20

Dear Heavenly Father:

Thou who holdest the universe in place and dost control all Thy works, we have felt the quaking of the earth and art reminded of our helplessness. Thou, O Lord God, art in charge and we submit ourselves to Thee, asking that Thou wilt have mercy upon us and keep us by Thy grace. *Amen.*

AUGUST 21

Dear Heavenly Father:
Thy Word is a lamp unto my feet and a light unto my pathway. The more I study Thy Word the more contemporary it is to me. It speaks to my condition. In it I find comfort. In it I find the reason not only for my own existence, but for Thy purpose in the life of all who trust in Thee. Help me truly to trust in Thy Word, and hold Thy promises firm. Guide me today, I pray. *Amen.*

AUGUST 22

Dear Heavenly Father:
Thou who knowest all and understandest all about us, I thank Thee that I can claim Thy love. Thou art all I need, and in Thee I am safe. Grant me a truly thankful heart and bolster my faith. Help me to follow Thee and praise Thee under all circumstances. Use me as Thou wilt, I pray. *Amen.*

AUGUST 23

Dear Heavenly Father:
I thank Thee that Thy mercy is everlasting unto me. I thank Thee that Thou art ever available to sustain and support, and that no matter what the circumstance, Thou art available to lead and guide. Help me this day to be ever mindful of Thy presence and draw me nearer to Thee. *Amen.*

AUGUST 24

Dear Heavenly Father:

To Thee be the glory, the honor, and the praise. It is good to know Thee and to know that Thou carest for me. I thank Thee, Lord, for all that Thou art. In this new day, I rejoice in Thee, for I feel Thy blessings upon me. Help me this day to praise Thee and glorify Thee. Use me as Thou wilt. *Amen.*

AUGUST 25

Dear Heavenly Father:

I thank Thee for another opportunity to praise Thee, for another moment to love Thee, for another day to be used by Thee. Fulfill Thy purpose in me and cause this part of Thy Kingdom to move a little further toward Thine expectation. In Thy dear Name, I pray. *Amen.*

AUGUST 26

Dear Heavenly Father:

I thank thee that Thou art in the future as much as Thou hast been in the past, and art in the present. I thank Thee that with Thee every moment is Thine. It is with that assurance and sense of Thy presence that I face this day knowing that Thou wilt be with me all the way. *Amen.*

AUGUST 27

Dear Heavenly Father:

I acknowledge Thee because Thou hast planted Thy Spirit within me. Thou hast revealed Thy love in the person of Jesus Christ, and hast saved me from the pangs of eternal death by establishing eternal life in Christ. Help me, Lord, to live in Thy life this day and forever. *Amen.*

AUGUST 28

Dear Heavenly Father:
I thank Thee for Thyself and all Thou art to me. Thou hast been mindful of me before my beginning, and hast been mindful of me ever since. I thank Thee, Lord, that Thou hast laid Thy hand on me and hast selected me to be a chosen vessel unto Thee. Grant me the wisdom and the grace to fulfill Thy plan, and to give Thee the glory. *Amen.*

AUGUST 29

Dear Heavenly Father:
Thou who art the Seat of all consciousness and the Source of all wisdom; Thou who hast imitated Thyself in Thy Son Jesus Christ in order that we may understand Thy Love; help me this day to live in Thee. Work Thy will in me and lead me in the path of truth. *Amen.*

AUGUST 30

Dear Heavenly Father:
Thou who knowest all and from whom no secrets are hid, I open my heart to Thee that Thine eternal love might fill me. Thou knowest, dear Lord, my desire to love Thee and serve Thee. So teach me Thy way that I may do Thy will. Guide me this day and help me to honor Thee. *Amen.*

AUGUST 31

Eternal and Our Ever-Loving God:
I thank Thee for Thy perfection and for the mighty pull toward Thee. I thank Thee that there is satisfaction in no other, and that Thou art always ready to receive those who call upon Thee in truth. Help me to abide in Thee so that I may be able to bring forth fruit worthy of Thy praise. *Amen.*

September

SEPTEMBER 1

Dear Heavenly Father:
I seek to do Thy will and not to take one step without Thine aid. Thou who hast charted the course of this day, lead me into Thy paths and help me to accomplish that which Thou hast designed. Eternal Father, hold Thou my hand and guide me in the paths of truth. Help me to honor Thee today. *Amen.*

SEPTEMBER 2

Eternal and Ever-Loving God:
I thank Thee for Thy creation and for Thy provision. I thank Thee that Thou hast made it possible for us to know Thee, and to find fulfillment in Thee. I know that Thou art kind to all, and Thou causest Thy goodness to fall on the just and the unjust, but Lord, I thank Thee that Thou didst save me. *Amen.*

SEPTEMBER 3

Dear Heavenly Father:
Thou who hast given Thy Son Jesus Christ to bring us to Thee, I thank Thee for the love and life that Christ revealed. I thank Thee for the privilege of calling Thee Father and for the hope of eternal life. Help me, Lord, to praise Thee for all that Thou art, and to serve Thee as long as I ought. *Amen.*

SEPTEMBER 4

Dear Heavenly Father:
Thou who hast planted in me the capacity for Thee, that longing that is not satisfied until I come to Thee and feel Thy presence within me. Dear Lord, I thank Thee for the inner comfort of Thy presence, no

matter what the outward circumstances. Thou who inhabitest eternity, whose Name is Holy, dwell Thou within my life today. *Amen.*

SEPTEMBER 5

Dear Heavenly Father:
I thank Thee once more for Thy goodness, O Lord, for Thy care and Thy tender mercies. If Thou desired sacrifice I would give it, but Thou askest only for a humble and contrite heart. Therefore, I come to Thee laying myself at Thy Throne, asking that Thou wilt receive me. *Amen.*

SEPTEMBER 6

Eternal Father:
Thou unto whom I can always come; Thou who wilt always receive me and incline Thine ear to me; I thank Thee for Thy love. I need Thee, O Lord, to guide me as I seek to do Thy will, declaring Thy goodness and proclaiming Thy Word. Help me in my living to be ever mindful of Thy presence. Use me this day. *Amen.*

SEPTEMBER 7

Eternal Father:
Giver of life, the Source of love, our eternal Comfort and our God, I thank Thee that I am privileged to come once more to praise Thee. I thank Thee that Thy love is everlasting and Thy truth endureth to all generations. Help me to obey Thy call and glorify Thy Name as I seek to do Thy will this day. *Amen.*

SEPTEMBER 8

Dear Eternal Father:
Thou who knowest me within and without; Thou who understandest my thoughts afar off and art acquainted with all my ways; Thou who

knowest me even more than I could know myself; I thank Thee for loving me even when I am unlovely. Use me this day, I pray. *Amen.*

SEPTEMBER 9

Dear Heavenly Father:
Maker of heaven and earth, Giver of life and all good gifts, Preserver of all who call upon Thee, I thank Thee for Thy goodness and Thy love. Thou who knowest all my desires; Thou who understandest all my thoughts; help me, O Lord, to follow Thy leading and do Thy will always. *Amen.*

SEPTEMBER 10

Eternal Father:
I thank Thee that through Thy grace it is possible for me to come to Thee; it is possible for me to call Thee Father; it is possible for me to claim Thee as friend. Thou who knowest my frame and understandest that I am dust, Thou hast seen fit to love me. Help me. O Lord, to serve Thee aright. *Amen.*

SEPTEMBER 11

Eternal Father:
Thou who hast established faith in me; Thou who hast allowed me to exercise that faith in Thee; Thou who hast given examples of the valiant who, in all odds, have held fast to Thee; continue to keep me close, dear Lord. Help me to declare Thee to my fellowmen so that they will see clearer that Thou art the God of love. *Amen.*

SEPTEMBER 12

Dear Heavenly Father:
This is a new day and I stand before Thee as a blank page, ready to be

filled with the indelible ink of Thy message. Imprint on me the story Thou desirest for this portion of the world and let me be faithful in delivering it for Thee. Use me as Thou wilt, I pray. *Amen.*

SEPTEMBER 13

Father God:
Thou who hast smiled upon us with Thy grace, and hast afforded us the privilege of claiming Thee as Lord, I thank Thee for Thy goodness, Thy care, Thy mercy. Help me to know and do Thy will. Help me to serve Thee in spirit and in truth. Walk with me and keep me close to Thee. *Amen.*

SEPTEMBER 14

Eternal and Ever-Loving Lord:
I come once more by Thy grace to thank Thee for Thyself, for the desire that Thou hast planted in me to be drawn near to Thee and love Thee. Thou who satisfiest my longing soul and givest purpose to all of life; Thou who hast manifested Thine abundance in all things; help me to praise Thee always. *Amen.*

SEPTEMBER 15

Eternal Father:
Giver of every good and perfect gift, Provider of the way whereby we can know Thee, Builder of Thy Kingdom in the hearts of mankind, Giver of life eternal to all who receive Thee, I thank Thee for all that Thou art in me, and I ask that Thou wilt fulfill Thy will in me. *Amen.*

SEPTEMBER 16

Dear Heavenly Father:
Giver of life, Author of love, Provider of mercy, Deliverer of grace; Thou who hast created us for Thyself, yet we have gone away as lost sheep; Thou whose goodness is still poured out upon us; dear Lord, help me this day to realize more fully Thy love for me. *Amen.*

SEPTEMBER 17

Eternal Father and Our God:
Thou who in Thy wisdom hast created us and granted us the capacity to receive Thee, I thank Thee for the gift of Thy Holy Spirit who comforteth, guideth, and teacheth us Thy will. I thank Thee, Lord, that no matter what the situation, Thou art there to be with us if we call upon Thee. Guide me this day, I ask. *Amen.*

SEPTEMBER 18

Dear Heavenly Father:
I come to Thee again to offer my thanks for all that Thou art, for Thy loving care of Thy servant, and for the peace and comfort I find in Thee. I thank Thee that in Thee is the fullness of all of life, and that all that I have to do is to trust Thee and walk humbly with Thee. Use me this day, I pray. *Amen.*

SEPTEMBER 19

Dear Heavenly Father:
I depend upon Thee for guidance. I need Thee every hour. I desire to do Thy will and to fulfill Thy plan for me. Help me, Lord, to know how to benefit from the guidance of Thy Holy Spirit, and grant me the grace to know, even when it is difficult, that Thou art with me. *Amen.*

SEPTEMBER 20

Dear Heavenly Father:

Thou who givest us the victory yet art glad to rejoice with us; Thou who hast made our hearts glad; I thank Thee, dear Lord, for the revelation of Thy love, for Thy care and all Thy goodness. My heart is grounded in Thee and my will is bent toward Thee. Make me truly Thine. *Amen.*

SEPTEMBER 21

Dear Heavenly Father:

Again I come to Thee to give Thee thanks for all Thy goodness toward me. All around me is evidence of Thy care and love. Thou art with me everywhere and Thy presence fills me with joy. Accept, I pray Thee, my heartfelt thanks, and help me in all things to honor Thee. *Amen.*

SEPTEMBER 22

Dear Heavenly Father:

Thou who hast granted more time in which I can praise Thee; Thou who hast showered more of Thy blessings so that I can enjoy; Thou who art working Thy purpose out so that all mankind will know and acknowledge Thee; for all these I thank Thee, Lord. *Amen.*

SEPTEMBER 23

Dear Heavenly Father:

It is good to trust in Thee, Thou who inhabiteth eternity, whose Name is Holy, who dwelleth in the high and holy place yet abideth in the heart of the contrite one. Thou in whom all things consist and who, in Thy great design, hast given me the privilege of worshiping Thee, be with me this day. *Amen.*

SEPTEMBER 24

Dear Heavenly Father:

Thou who hast made us to know Thee and hast given us the will and the desire to seek after Thee; Thou who hast made us restless until we find Thee; I thank Thee for the revelation of Thyself in the person of Thy Son, Jesus Christ. Breathe again Thy Holy Spirit upon me and help me to love Thee. *Amen.*

SEPTEMBER 25

Dear Heavenly Father:

Thy Word is real, Thy Word is true. I shall not be afraid, for my heart is fixed trusting in Thee. Grant me wisdom, Lord, to meet each situation in Thy Spirit. Grant me grace to conduct myself in ways that are honorable in Thy sight. Grant me love that I will represent Thee in my living. *Amen.*

SEPTEMBER 26

Dear Heavenly Father:

I thank Thee for choosing me to be a part of Thy plan. Help me to fully interpret the meaning of Thy purpose as it is presented to me today. Grant me wisdom, knowledge, and understanding to do that which will please Thee, and take the praise to Thyself, I pray. *Amen.*

SEPTEMBER 27

Dear Heavenly Father:

For the beauty of the earth, for the glory of the skies, for the love which from my birth over and around me lies, I thank Thee, Lord. For all Thy goodness and Thy care, for all Thy promises and Thy plan, for all the possibilities that are in Thee for me, I give Thee thanks. Use me as Thou wilt this day. *Amen.*

SEPTEMBER 28

Dear Heavenly Father:

We do not understand why tragedies happen. We become confused about how much control Thou exercisest over all things at all times. We do not have all the answers. However, Lord, Thou hast taught us to trust Thee, and Thou hast given us the example of Jesus. So keep us in Thy grace, I pray. *Amen.*

SEPTEMBER 29

Dear Heavenly Father:

I thank Thee that Thou knowest what is best for me and through Thy Holy Spirit Thou leadest me to it. So often the path is long and hard and doubt fills my mind. Yet, Thou never leavest nor forsakest, and in the end I can rejoice in Thy leading. Guide me this day, I pray. *Amen.*

SEPTEMBER 30

Dear Heavenly Father:

I need Thee always, and in Thy faithfulness Thou makest Thyself available and manifestesteth Thy love in a multitude of ways. Thy goodness is everlasting and Thy truth endureth to all generations. Continue to keep me in Thy plan and grant me the wisdom and strength to do Thy will. *Amen.*

OCTOBER

OCTOBER 1

Dear Heavenly Father:

Thou who hast numbered my days and hast charted my course, I thank Thee that Thou art also beside me to guide me all the way. Thou who art closer than breathing and nearer than hands and feet, I pledge again my life to serve Thee, and ask that Thou wouldst be pleased to use me. *Amen.*

OCTOBER 2

Eternal Father:

Grant me the right attitude, the proper words, and the submissive will to pray to Thee. I seek only to fulfill that which Thou desirest, so use me in Thy service. Grant me the wisdom to follow Thy leading and keep my mind tuned to Thee. *Amen.*

OCTOBER 3

Dear Heavenly Father:

I thank Thee again for all Thy love and mercy bestowed upon me. I thank Thee that Thou art ever mindful of me, and art always willing to answer my call. Keep me near to Thee this day, and grant me opportunity to serve Thee fully. Lead me in the path of righteousness, I pray. *Amen.*

OCTOBER 4

Dear Heavenly Father:

Thou who hast promised to grant us Thy Holy Spirit, who will teach us all things and who will make intercession for us, I claim Thy promise and thank Thee for Thy goodness. Help me to fulfill Thy will and be faithful unto Thee. *Amen.*

OCTOBER 5

Dear Heavenly Father:

I thank Thee for Thy goodness and care, Thy tender mercies and Thy love. I thank Thee that Thou knowest all things, and that Thou hast promised that no good thing Thou wilt withhold from anyone who trusts Thee. Accept my thanksgiving and help me to serve Thee. *Amen.*

OCTOBER 6

Eternal Father:

Thou who art order and hast established within us the sense of order, help me this day to be governed by Thee. Help me to yield my will to Thee, that that which is purposed by Thee might come to pass as Thou wilt. Lead me, Lord, in the path of righteousness for Thy Name's sake. *Amen.*

OCTOBER 7

Dear Heavenly Father:

I again reflect upon the mystery of the Cross, the path Thou hast chosen to bring salvation to mankind, such an unlikely gateway to eternal freedom and everlasting life. Yet, Thy power and Thy grace have brought us victory, and now in Jesus we are free forevermore. I thank Thee, Lord. *Amen.*

OCTOBER 8

Dear Heavenly Father:

It is a good thing to give thanks unto Thee. My heart is glad because I have this privilege. I come again to Thee, knowing that Thou art willing to hear me. Thou knowest the desires of my heart, and I ask that Thou wilt answer in Thine own time and in Thine own way. Help me to trust Thee and to praise Thee. *Amen.*

OCTOBER 9

Eternal Father:
Thou who hast revealed unto us to know the difference between the things that are temporal and those that are eternal; the things that are natural and those that are spiritual; the things that will last for a time and those that will last forever; help me this day to concentrate on eternal values. *Amen*

OCTOBER 10

Dear Heavenly Father:
I thank Thee for Thy many blessings. I claim victory in Thee and pledge to Thee my all. Help me to know how to praise Thee, O Lord. Grant me opportunity to glorify Thee for all that Thou art to me and mine. Use us as Thou wilt, O Lord, and fulfill Thy purpose in us. *Amen.*

OCTOBER 11

Dear Heavenly Father:
I can feel the progress in my body—I thank Thee for Thy help. As I am helped physically, I am also aware of my being helped mentally and spiritually. I depend on Thee, O Lord, for all Thy goodness, and I am grateful that Thou hearest and answerest prayers. Keep me close to Thee this day, I pray. *Amen.*

OCTOBER 12

Dear Heavenly Father:
Thou who hast designed it all and hast purposed that I be a part of Thy creation, I thank Thee for thinking of me and for providing for me so well. Long before I could even think of what I would need for situations, Thou already hast provided. Lead me this day to greater praise. *Amen.*

OCTOBER 13

Dear Heavenly Father:

Thou who art real to me; Thou who stimulatest me toward good, and givest me strength for each day's task; I thank Thee that Thou art near. Help me to properly interpret Thy message to me, and help me to follow Thy leading. Use me as Thou wilt this day, I pray. *Amen.*

OCTOBER 14

Dear Heavenly Father:

Thou who hast given us so many gifts that we may express Thy wonderful works; Thou who hast given us the evidence of eternity that we might seek after the permanent; guide me this day so that, as I live, Thine everlasting truth will be reflected in my life, and I will bear testimony to eternity. *Amen.*

OCTOBER 15

Eternal Father:

Thou who hast created within me a thirst after righteousness, and preparest the way for me to seek and find Thee; Thou who grantest fulfillment and peace unto those who have found Thee; I thank Thee, Lord, for the satisfaction which comes from Thee. Guide me this day to an even fuller appreciation of Thy goodness. *Amen.*

OCTOBER 16

Dear Heavenly Father:

Thou who, in Thy love, hast limited Thyself and given unto us freedom of choice—the freedom that allows us even not to choose Thee; Thou who hast made Thy love so available; I thank Thee. I have chosen Thee, O God, and have found in Thee the answer to all my needs. Make me truly grateful, and receive my thanks this day. *Amen.*

OCTOBER 17

Eternal Father:
Thou in whom we live and move and have our being; Thou who hast ordained our whole existence and hast planted within us a desire for Thee; I thank Thee, Lord, that I have the privilege of knowing Thee. Thy Spirit beareth witness within me and assureth me of Thy presence. Help me this day to show forth Thy love. *Amen.*

OCTOBER 18

Eternal God:
Thou who findest expression in all areas of Thy creation; Thou who hast brought into being the tiniest and the greatest of Thy creatures; Thou didst also bring me forth, and hast planted in me the capacity for Thee. That longing brings me to Thee now, and I thank Thee for Thy love. Use me as Thou wilt this day. *Amen.*

OCTOBER 19

Dear Heavenly Father:
Thou who givest strength in adversity; Thou who givest hope in despair; I thank Thee that I can come to Thee and share with Thee even those things Thou knowest about much more than I can ever know. Grant me the faith to know that all things work together for good in Thee. *Amen.*

OCTOBER 20

Dear Heavenly Father:
I thank Thee for the challenges of life. I thank Thee that Thou hast seen fit to choose me for these responsibilities. Grant me the strength and the wisdom to handle all the tasks that are given to me this day. Be near to me, O Lord, and fill me with Thy wisdom. *Amen.*

OCTOBER 21

Dear Heavenly Father:
I thank Thee that Thou art a God who answers prayers. I thank Thee that Thou art not too far removed from listening to my plea and granting relief. Dear Lord, I thank Thee that Thou knowest me within and without, and that Thou carest for me. Use me as Thou wilt, I pray. *Amen.*

OCTOBER 22

Dear Heavenly Father:
Thy mercy is everlasting and Thy truth endureth to all generations. I thank Thee that Thou hast made known Thy goodness toward me, and Thou hast preserved me unto Thy work. I regard it a privilege to participate in Thy purpose, and pray that Thou wilt have Thy way with me. *Amen.*

OCTOBER 23

Dear Heavenly Father:
Thou who knowest my frame and understandest that I am dust; Thou who art my God; I come once more to thank Thee for whom Thou art. I thank Thee that Thou art more mindful of me than I can be of myself. Help me to know Thy will for my life, and grant me the wisdom to fulfill Thy purpose for me. *Amen.*

OCTOBER 24

Dear Heavenly Father:
We are mindful of the bounty Thou hast poured upon us. Help us to hear Thy call to feed the hungry and clothe the naked. Grant us Thy grace in knowing how to do Thy will. *Amen.*

OCTOBER 25

Eternal Father:

Thou who hast done for me more than I could have thought or asked; Thou whose bounty is everlasting and whose truth endureth to all generations; I thank Thee for Thy goodness and Thy love. I thank Thee for the opportunity to love and serve Thee. Guide me this day, I pray. *Amen.*

OCTOBER 26

Eternal Father:

Thou whom I claim and have found faithful; Thou who hast promised that if we remain faithful unto death, Thou wilt give a crown of life; this day is another gift of Thy stream of life, and I pray that Thou wilt help me to serve Thee aright today. Use me as Thou wilt. *Amen.*

OCTOBER 27

Eternal Father:

Thou who art strong to save and to grant Thy grace to whom Thou wilt; Thou who hast promised that whosoever cometh unto Thee, Thou wilt in no wise cast out; Thou who art closer than breathing and nearer than hands and feet; be with me this day and help me to do Thy will. *Amen.*

OCTOBER 28

Dear Heavenly Father:

We thank Thee for the vision that Thou didst give to those who discovered this land. I thank Thee for the opportunities that this country affords. Help us, dear Lord, to realize the privileges we have to serve Thee and our fellow man. Guide me this day, I pray. *Amen.*

OCTOBER 29

Eternal Father:

Once more it is my privilege to come to Thee and lay my thanksgiving on Thine altar. Thou who art more mindful of me than I can be of myself; Thou who knowest my thoughts afar off and art acquainted with all my ways; I desire to worship Thee in my living, so be Thou my Guide, I pray. *Amen.*

OCTOBER 30

Eternal Father:

I thank Thee for Thy preservation, Thy care, Thy mercies, and Thy love. Thou who canst be trusted at all times and in all things, I thank Thee for the joy of knowing Thee and for the privilege of coming to Thee at any time and place. Guide me this day and help me in doing Thy will. *Amen.*

OCTOBER 31

Eternal Father:

I rejoice in Thy goodness and Thy care. I am glad for Thine ever-binding comfort. I feel so refreshed when I have the privilege of drawing near to Thee. I remember Thy promise that Thou wilt never leave us nor forsake us. Dear Lord, help me this day to live for Thee. *Amen.*

November

NOVEMBER 1

Eternal Father:

Thou who givest varying experiences to build us up to understand that Thou canst be with us; Thou who art able to sustain, keep, and comfort us and make us know that Thou art always with us; I thank Thee for Thine everlasting love. Help me this day to do Thy will and praise Thee. *Amen.*

NOVEMBER 2

Dear Heavenly Father:

Thou in whom all things consist and who knowest the ways of all Thy servants; Thou who hast given us the capacity to know Thee and worship Thee; Thou who hast blessed us with knowledge to discover Thy purpose; grant me this day the wisdom necessary to live for Thee. *Amen.*

NOVEMBER 3

Dear Heavenly Father:

Thou who hast established friendship and the joy that comes from fellowship; Thou who desirest that Thy people should dwell together in unity; I thank Thee, Lord, that it is my privilege to have friends and to know that Thou art the greatest friend of all. *Amen.*

NOVEMBER 4

Dear Heavenly Father:

Thou who hast granted the capacity to think, so that out of thinking we can bring forth deeds to fulfill Thy divine purpose, grant me this day those creative thoughts that will advance the quality of actions that will speed Thy Kingdom on earth. Let Thy Holy Spirit lead me this day, I pray. *Amen.*

NOVEMBER 5

Dear Heavenly Father:
Thou who art the Source of all being, the Orderer of existence; Thou who knowest the intricacies of all that Thy hand hath made and who knowest me fully; I thank Thee that Thou canst assess my desire to love and serve Thee. Use me this day as Thou wilt and help me in all things to honor Thee. *Amen.*

NOVEMBER 6

Dear Heavenly Father:
Thou hast made it possible for me to come to Thee. Thou hast said whosoever cometh unto Thee, Thou wilt in no wise cast out. This open invitation, although available to all, is acceptable only by a few. Dear Lord, I thank Thee that Thou hast revealed Thyself to me, and again I lay myself upon Thine altar of service. *Amen.*

NOVEMBER 7

Eternal Father:
To Thee I come, knowing that Thou knowest all things, and that Thou understandest me even more than I can understand myself. Thou who hast established and directed my way, lead me to Thy path of peace. Cause me, O Lord, to rejoice in Thee. *Amen.*

NOVEMBER 8

Dear Heavenly Father:
Thou who hast granted me grace; Thou who mysteriously provides for me in ways beyond my imagining; Thou who pourest out Thy love and Thy grace toward me; help me, dear Lord, to be ever mindful of Thy goodness and seek to do Thy will. Guide me this day and help me to praise Thee. *Amen.*

NOVEMBER 9

Dear Heavenly Father:

I thank Thee for strength and for the privilege of relying on Thee from whom cometh this strength. Thou hast promised that those who trust in Thee shall be as Mount Zion, and I depend on Thee to keep me close to Thee. Guide me today and grant me Thy grace to love and serve Thee. *Amen.*

NOVEMBER 10

Dear Heavenly Father:

I thank Thee that Thou art always there when we call, that Thou workest out ways to satisfy our needs, and to let us be assured that we are in Thy love and care. Have Thy way with me this day, and help me in all things to know Thee. *Amen.*

NOVEMBER 11

Eternal Father:

Creator of all and Preserver of Thy servant, Thy ways are past finding out. The intricacy of Thy plan surpasses the comprehension of the mind of man. I thank Thee, Lord, that Thou hast made known Thy love, and that I can know assuredly that I am Thy child. Guide me today and help me to do Thy will. *Amen.*

NOVEMBER 12

Dear Heavenly Father:

I thank Thee for Thy grace. Thou art so patient with me and seek to guide me to understand Thy way. Lead me in the path of righteousness this day, and help that, even in the common round, I will be mindful of Thy presence. Help me to abide in Thee, O Lord, this day and forever. *Amen.*

November 13

Our Father God:
Creator, Reclaimer, Provider, and Friend, Thou who art nearer than breathing and closer than hands and feet, live through me this day and fill me with the sense of Thy purpose. Grant me Thy grace, O Lord, and help me to follow Thee. *Amen.*

November 14

Dear Heavenly Father:
I thank Thee for another birthday and for Thy keeping care and tender mercies of the past years. I dedicate myself again to Thy service and pray that Thou wilt grant me wisdom, knowledge, and understanding in the years ahead. Use me as Thou wilt, I pray. *Amen.*

November 15

Dear Heavenly Father:
Thou whom I can trust in all things to do good, Thou seest and knowest the needs of this day. Have Thy perfect way and do Thy perfect will, and by Thy divine grace, help me to be a part of Thy Holy purpose. *Amen.*

November 16

Dear Heavenly Father:
Another day of credit to Thy bounty, and I thank Thee. To know that Thou hast all my days in Thy hand, and that Thou chartest my course even until I reach Thy harbor, is satisfying to me. I pray that this will be another day when I can praise Thee. Help me to count the evidences of Thy goodness and magnify Thy Name. *Amen.*

NOVEMBER 17

Dear Heavenly Father:

I come once more to praise Thee for being mindful of me and granting me Thy Holy Spirit. I am grateful for the privilege of knowing Thee and of benefiting from Thy bounty. I thank Thee for Thy promise that Thou wilt keep me in perfect peace as I rest in Thee. Use me as Thou wilt, I pray, this day. *Amen.*

NOVEMBER 18

Eternal Father:

Thou who sustainest us in the race of life, and Thou who art the prize, help me this day to fix my gaze on Thee. Strengthen me, so that I will be able to press on toward the mark of the high calling and be crowned by Thee. *Amen.*

NOVEMBER 19

Dear Heavenly Father:

Thou who art the Fount of goodness and love; Thou on whom I can depend; I come once more to Thee just as I am. Thou knowest, Lord; Thou understandest my needs, my desires, my hopes; make them all worthy of Thee. Help me, O Lord, to know how to love Thee, and help me to praise Thy Name. *Amen.*

NOVEMBER 20

Dear Heavenly Father:

Thou who knowest all about me and understandest all my desires, I bring all of me to Thee once more to ask that Thou wilt sanctify and make me worthy for Thyself. I thank Thee for the privilege of knowing Thee and claiming Thee as God and Savior. I thank Thee for the victories of the past, and trust Thee for the future victories as I yield myself to doing Thy will *Amen.*

NOVEMBER 21

Eternal Father:
Thou who hast granted me purpose and hast prospered my way; Thou who hast designed my path and led me all the way; hold my hand, O Lord, and help me never to feel that I am alone at any time. Guide me into the path of truth and help me to do Thy will. *Amen.*

NOVEMBER 22

Dear Heavenly Father:
I thank Thee that Thou carest even for the very little things. I thank Thee that nothing is too small for Thee to care about. I thank Thee that Thou carest about every part of me. In marvelous ways Thou hast shown Thy love, and I am grateful to Thee. Use me as Thou wilt, I pray. *Amen.*

NOVEMBER 23

Dear Heavenly Father:
Thou who art a God of mercy; Thou who understandest the needs of all Thy children; look down with compassion on us at this time. Dear Lord, I trust Thee; Thou art our only real Source of help. Thou knowest our hearts that we depend upon Thee. Help me to praise Thee continually and to do Thy will. *Amen.*

NOVEMBER 24

Eternal Father:
Thou who bringest us into dimensions beyond our imaginings; Thou who openest doors of possibilities as we yield ourselves to Thee; fill

me this day with Thy promise, that I may reveal Thy goodness to Thy children. Help me truly to serve Thee, O Lord. *Amen.*

NOVEMBER 25

Dear Heavenly Father:
Thanksgiving is given unto Thee for all that Thou art to me. Thanksgiving is given unto Thee for all that Thou hast promised unto me. Thanksgiving is given unto Thee for all that Thou hast accomplished within me. Thanksgiving is given unto Thee for all that I will become in Thee. *Amen.*

NOVEMBER 26

Dear Heavenly Father:
For this, another privilege to come to Thee, I thank Thee. Thou who knowest all that this day contains, and art already at the end of the day, I depend on Thee for guidance, strength, knowledge, and love to meet all that comes my way. Help me, Lord, to serve Thee with all my heart. *Amen.*

NOVEMBER 27

Dear Heavenly Father:
For the continuing mystery of life in Thee, I thank Thee. Thou who art always filling me with wonder and praise; Thou about whom there are always satisfying discoveries and reason for joy; I thank Thee. Lead me this day toward even greater appreciation of Thy love and goodness. In Thy Name, I pray. *Amen.*

NOVEMBER 28

Dear Heavenly Father:
There is no disappointment in Thee, and although I cannot see the

whole issue, and do not know the hidden parts, I trust Thee and know that Thou who knowest all things will work all things well. Thank Thee, Lord, for Thy goodness. *Amen.*

NOVEMBER 29

Dear Heavenly Father:
I thank Thee for the inspiration of Thy Holy Spirit and for the joy that Thou givest. I thank Thee that Thou wilt never leave me nor forsake me, and that every day with Thee is sweeter than the day before. Help me this day to know more of Thy will for me, and grant me the grace to accomplish that which Thou desirest. *Amen.*

NOVEMBER 30

Dear Heavenly Father:
I thank Thee for Thyself and for the many blessings Thou hast bestowed upon me. I thank Thee that Thou art always working ways whereby I can praise Thee. Use me, O Lord, in the ways Thou knowest I can serve Thee best, and grant me the Spirit that will glorify Thy Name. Lead me this day as Thou wilt. *Amen.*

DECEMBER

December 1

Dear Heavenly Father:

I thank Thee that Thou hast the answer to all my questions and the solutions to all life's problems. As I live today, help me to cast all my cares upon Thee, for Thou carest for me and Thou lovest me. Grant me Thy Holy Spirit, O Lord, and help me to serve Thee. *Amen.*

December 2

Dear Heavenly Father:

Thou whom Jesus hath made plain and hath invited all mankind to worship; Thou who art the God of love, and who seekest all Thy creation to honor Thee; I come once more to praise and adore Thee, to thank Thee for all Thou hast been to me and mine. I pledge to Thee my all. Use me as Thou wilt. *Amen.*

December 3

Dear Heavenly Father:

I thank Thee for Thy goodness and Thy mercy. I thank Thee for an ever clearer knowledge of Thy working in the world. Thou art our Lord and our Keeper; Thou desirest our devotion. Lead me into the paths of righteousness, and help me to honor Thee. Grant me Thy peace this day, and help me to praise Thee. *Amen.*

December 4

Dear Heavenly Father:

I know by Thy provision that Thou lovest me. I know by Thy gifts that Thou carest. I know by Thy promises that Thou wilt be faithful. I know by Thy mercy that I am saved. Use me this day, O Lord, to do Thy will. Guide me as I seek to follow Thee. *Amen.*

DECEMBER 5

Dear Heavenly Father:

All that I am I give to Thee—all that Thou wilt let me be. Grant me Thy grace to do Thy will, and receive the praise which comes to Thee. I thank Thee, dear Lord, for all that Thou art. Please lead me in doing what Thou desirest. *Amen.*

DECEMBER 6

Eternal Father:

I thank Thee that as long as Thou grantest the gift of life there is always another chance to come to Thee and acknowledge Thy goodness and Thy love. There is always a new beginning with Thee, so make this day one in which I will discover anew Thy love. *Amen.*

DECEMBER 7

Dear Heavenly Father:

Thou who guidest and protectest and keepest me from evil; Thou who watchest over me all the days; Thou who hast promised to keep me as the apple of Thine eye; I thank Thee. Help me this day to be even more aware of Thy goodness, and grant me the heart of praise. Help me to honor Thee in all I do. In Thy dear Name, I pray. *Amen.*

DECEMBER 8

Dear Heavenly Father:

I thank Thee that Thou art in charge and that Thou hast the plan for all of us in Thy command. I yield myself again to Thee, praying that Thou wilt have mercy and lead me in Thy path. Help me to know and do Thy will. In all my doings help me to praise Thee. *Amen.*

DECEMBER 9

Dear Heavenly Father:

Thou who restorest the faint and offerest strength to those who are weak; Thou who art the Source of life, and shall be the Sustainer of all who trust in Thee; I thank Thee for the privilege of knowing Thee, and for the joy of claiming Thee. I am Thine, O Lord, so use me as Thou wilt in accomplishing Thy purpose. *Amen.*

DECEMBER 10

Dear Heavenly Father:

I thank Thee for another opportunity to praise Thee; for the warmth of the sun, although it is winter. Thy glory is continuous, and we can see Thy glory shine through all the gloom, if only we allow Thee to have Thy way with us. Thank Thee for this season when we can remember Thy coming to earth in Jesus. Help me to love Thee, I pray. *Amen.*

DECEMBER 11

Dear Heavenly Father:

I thank Thee for Thy continued blessings, for the privilege of knowing Thee, and for the joy that I receive from Thee. Help me to fulfill Thy will for my life. Guide me in the paths of righteousness, and lead me to live the truth of Thy message. I yield again myself to Thee to serve as Thou desirest. *Amen.*

DECEMBER 12

Eternal Father:

Thou who orderest Thy world after Thine own design, and placest in line the times and the seasons to accomplish Thy plan; Thou who art constant and changest not, yet answerest the cry of Thy changing ones;

be near to me this day and guide me in the path of righteousness, that I may praise Thee. *Amen.*

DECEMBER 13

Dear Heavenly Father:
Thou who art eternal Love and hast expressed that love in the person of Jesus Christ; who hast shown us the meaning of being the Suffering Servant as well as the Victorious King; I thank Thee for this mystery. I know that Thou hast laid Thy hand on me, so help me to live for Thee. Guide me this day, I pray. *Amen.*

DECEMBER 14

Dear Heavenly Father:
Thou who art always near; Thou who knowest me within and without; I thank Thee, Lord, for Thy preservation and for Thy goodness. Help me to live for Thee and accomplish that for which Thou hast brought me into being. Grant me the wisdom to do Thy will, and cause me always to praise Thee. *Amen.*

DECEMBER 15

Dear Lord:
Thou who hast made Thyself real through Thy Word; Thou who hast spoken in times past through the prophets and through Thy Son Jesus Christ; speak through Thy Holy Spirit to my heart today, and help me to honor Thee. *Amen.*

DECEMBER 16

Dear Heavenly Father:
Thou who holdest our time in Thy hand and determinest the number of our days; Thou who purposest our plan and grantest unto us the

strength to fulfill it; I thank Thee that it is not left up to me to order my day, so once more I give myself to Thee to fill me with Thy Spirit and use me as Thou wilt. *Amen.*

DECEMBER 17

Dear Heavenly Father:
For the privilege of life, I give Thee thanks. For the intricacy of the senses, I praise Thy Name. For the gift of awareness and the blessings of Thy presence, I thank Thee, Lord. Fill me with Thy Holy Spirit this day and help me to show forth Thy love. Lead me in the path of service for Thee. *Amen.*

DECEMBER 18

Dear Heavenly Father:
Thou who hast showered us with rain and, in due time, bringest out the sun; Thou who orderest the seasons and keepest in place all the planets and the constellations; keep my days within Thy plan and cause me to fulfill Thy will. Help me in all things to praise Thee and in all my living to honor Thee. *Amen.*

DECEMBER 19

Dear Heavenly Father:
Thou who hast granted me the spirit of discernment to be able to desire Thee, I thank Thee. Help me always to choose Thy way and walk in Thy path. It is so safe to be with Thee, O Lord, and to know that Thou keepest not only now but unto the end of the world. *Amen.*

DECEMBER 20

Dear Heavenly Father:
Thou who makest me happy; Thou who makest me glad; Thou who

bringest real joy; Thou who receivest thanksgiving; I offer to Thee the best that I have, asking that Thou wilt be pleased to receive my all. Use me as Thou wilt, O Lord, and help me in all things to praise Thy Name. *Amen.*

DECEMBER 21

Dear Heavenly Father:

I thank Thee that Thou dost provide for all my needs, that Thou dost consider me even when I am not thinking of myself. I thank Thee, Lord, that Thou hast made all Thy children Thy primary concern and that those who trust in Thee shall not want any good thing. Help me to praise Thee. *Amen.*

DECEMBER 22

Dear Heavenly Father:

Grant me Thy grace and help me to know and do Thy will. Lead me in the paths of righteousness and give me the wisdom and strength to be faithful to Thy truth. I need Thee every hour, most gracious Lord. Help me to feel Thee near as I seek to follow Thee. *Amen.*

DECEMBER 23

Our Father God:

Thou who hast revealed Thyself in the person of Thy Son Jesus Christ our Lord; Thou who hast promised that whatsoever we ask in His Name Thou wilt grant; I come to Thee this day to request that Thou wilt have Thy way in my life, and grant me the grace to do Thy will. *Amen.*

DECEMBER 24

Dear Heavenly Father:

Thou who, in the fullness of time, sent Thy Son Jesus Christ to redeem those of us who were under the law of sin; I thank Thee, Lord, for this redemption and for the joy of salvation. Be born anew in me again this Christmas season and help me to reveal Thy goodness. *Amen.*

DECEMBER 25

Dear Heavenly Father:

I thank Thee for the joy of Christmas and for the opportunity of appreciating the snow and the cold; for the benefit of a warm building and the many decorations and cards; for the love of the people around; and most of all, for Jesus Christ who came to redeem us. *Amen.*

DECEMBER 26

Dear Heavenly Father:

I thank Thee that, through Jesus, Thou art approachable. I am grateful for thy goodness and care, for Thy healing touch and Thy tender mercies. Help me to rely upon Thee at all times and in all things, knowing that in Thee is true fulfillment. *Amen.*

DECEMBER 27

Dear Heavenly Father:

I thank Thee that Thou hast bidden us to come to Thee—that Thou hast promised that, before we call, Thou wilt answer, and while we are speaking, Thou wilt hear. I come again to Thee, knowing that Thou knowest and understandest all my needs. I trust Thee to bring to pass for my good that which Thou wilt. *Amen.*

DECEMBER 28

Dear Heavenly Father:

Thou in whom I live and breathe and have my being; Thou who art my all in all; Thou to whom I can come with any concern and Thou turnest not away; Thou who satisfiest; I thank Thee for all that Thou art. Grant that all my days will be spent praising Thee. Help me today to know and do Thy will. *Amen.*

DECEMBER 29

Dear Heavenly Father:
Help me to be ever conscious of Thy goodness and Thy love. Thou who hast given unto me all that is necessary to praise Thee, dear Lord, Thy bounty is always toward me, and I feel Thy Spirit welling up within me. Keep me near, this day, I pray. *Amen.*

DECEMBER 30

Dear Heavenly Father:
My heart finds rest when I come to Thee in prayer. I feel that love enfolds me as I understand the meaning of Thy Word, "Lo, I am with thee always unto the end of the world." Keep me conscious of Thy Presence this day. *Amen.*

DECEMBER 31

Dear Heavenly Lord:
I thank Thee that Thou hast given me another opportunity to lift my thoughts in praise to Thee for all Thy goodness to me. I thank Thee, Father, that this world belongs to Thee and, no matter what we do to it, Thou art still in charge, and Thou art working Thy purpose out as year succeeds to year. Hasten the time when we shall experience Thy full glory. *Amen.*

ABOUT THE AUTHOR

Noel Palmer is a recorded Minister of the Religious Society of Friends (Quakers). He has pastored Meetings in his native island of Jamaica WI, and has also pastored the Manhattan Monthly Meeting in New York City.

Noel is a retired educational administrator for the State University of New York, where he served for twenty-three years. He has written two books: *Daily Notes To God* as well as *Westbury Friends School: The First Forty Years.*

DAILY NOTES TO GOD ONLINE!

2011 marks the 20th anniversary of the publication of *Daily Notes to God* by Noel Palmer. In 1991, *Daily Notes to God* made Pastor Palmer's morning reflections for every day of the year available in print form to book readers, encouraging them to add their own daily reflections and prayers at the end.

With the re-publication of Pastor Palmer's book, *Daily Notes to God* has exploded in exciting new directions that are only available in the second decade of the 21st century. In addition to a new print version, Daily Notes to God is now available in digital format for Kindle and other e-readers, so readers may draw inspiration from Pastor Palmer's Notes even on-the-go. The book's website, *www.DailyNotesToGod.com*, offers audio recordings of Noel Palmer's sermons, available for download, for those who prefer to listen. And the site also includes an interactive blog that encourages visitors to share their own insights, reflections, and prayers. Harnessing the new possibilities offered by technological advances, *Daily Notes to God* is now an interactive forum for shared devotion and multiplying the praises of God.